YOU CAN'T WEAR OUT
AN INDIAN SCOUT

Showtime!

YOU CAN'T WEAR OUT AN INDIAN SCOUT

INDIANS & THE WALL OF DEATH

ALLAN FORD & NICK CORBLE

AMBERLEY

DEDICATION

To all those heroes who have devoted their life to entertain the public on the straight walled track and spent their lives trying to wear out their Indian Scout.

First published 2009
Amberley Publishing
Cirencester Road, Chalford,
Stroud, Gloucestershire, GL6 8PE

www.amberley-books.com

Copyright © Allan Ford & Nick Corble 2009

The right of Allan Ford & Nick Corble to be identified as the Authors of this work has been asserted in accordance with the Copyrights, Designs and Patents Act 1988.

ISBN 978 1 84868 094 4

British Library Cataloguing in Publication Data.
A catalogue record for this book is available from the British Library.

Typeset in 9pt on 13pt Sabon.
Typesetting and origination byAmberley Publishing.

Printed in the UK.

CONTENTS

Kerry Cameron riding The Rollers.

INTRODUCTION

There's something unique about the Wall of Death and the place it occupies in both the history of outdoor entertainment and in the memory of anyone who's ever been lucky enough to see one in action. Beyond the thrills and spills of the show however lies another equally special relationship, one between those who ride the Wall and the Indian Motorcycle. Despite not being produced in commercial quantities for over half a century, Indians are synonymous with the Wall, especially the very early 1920s models which every Wall of Death rider will tell you is the machine you want to trust your life to when hurtling round the perpendicular surface the Wall presents.

After achieving a lifetime's ambition to record the history of the Wall in 2006 with our book 'Riding the Wall of Death', it seemed natural to us that we should complete the story by following it up with another that looked into this special relationship between bike and rider, and this book is the result. Its title is drawn from an old saying from Sammy Pierce, a US Indian distributor, in what was both a testament to the Indian's robustness and at the same time a sly dig at their rivals the Harleys, and the efforts of Wall riders over more than half a century have proven his words to be true. Today, Indians of antique vintage continue to be ridden by Wall riders with a tribe of Indian enthusiasts sitting behind them keeping the Indian spirit alive and this book looks at why these bikes continue to hold their fascination for both groups.

It's also the story of how the relationship between Indian and the Wall developed and where it is now – not just in the UK but worldwide, with the story contained within these covers taking the reader from the US to the UK and Europe, Africa, the Middle, Near and Far East and Australia.

Allan Ford holds a special place in Wall of Death history, being the man who single-handedly rescued the Wall from obscurity in the UK in the 1980s, laying the foundations for what has become a revival of interest in the attraction. Nick Corble is the author of sixteen books, including 'Riding the Wall of Death' which he co-authored with Allan.

Finally, this book would not have been possible without the help and advice freely given by so many Indian enthusiasts. Special mention must go to Mike and Sybil de Bidalph and the Indian Riders Club, Charles Winter, Ken Fox and his family, but others have also made valuable contributions including Ray and Carol Cris, various members of the Messham family, Ned Kelly, John Richardson and Andy Donald. Any omissions and errors are entirely ours, but we hope these will be forgiven as a small price to pay for being given the chance to record the history of the Indians and the Wall of Death.

Allan Ford (www.thewallofdeath.com)
Nick Corble (www.nickcorble.co.uk)

Charley Boorman with the Ken Fox Troupe.

CHAPTER 1

OUT OF THE WIGWAM

When two men with contrasting qualities but a similar vision come together they can achieve remarkable things, much more than they could ever realise apart. In the world of cars the names Rolls and Royce come immediately to mind, and in the world of motorcycles the two standout candidates are George M. Hendee and Carl Oscar Hedstrom.

Hendee was born in 1866 to a family of Spanish origin, and grew up during a time when the bicycle was the preferred means of transport if you needed to get somewhere quicker than your feet could carry you and you didn't own a horse. The Hendees were retailers and in his teenage years George developed an interest in bicycles that developed to a point where, in 1886, when he was 20, he won the National Amateur High Wheel Championship, a title he retained for six years before turning professional. Bicycle racing was a huge sport at the time and George gained an enviable reputation, winning over 300 races during the course of his career, before retiring in 1895 after a brief and unsuccessful marriage.

George remained faithful to his first love, the bicycle, and proceeded to make a living as a salesman for various manufacturers. This allowed him to build up a good network of contacts, and valuable experience gained in travelling the country helped to foster a growing taste for business. In 1897 he decided to set up his own bicycle manufacturing plant in Springfield, Massachusetts, a choice of location informed in part by the location of the Springfield Armoury, home of the Springfield rifle, which in turn meant a good pool of skilled light engineers. Using his savings and $5,000 borrowed from a local bank, Hendee developed bicycle models built up at first from bought-in components and later using parts produced in-house.

Hendee continued to exercise his salesmanship and business skills in drumming up orders and publicising his bicycles, including the sponsoring of young riders on the professional circuit and by taking a stake in the newly opened Springfield Coliseum racing track. As the new century turned such was his success that he was able to buy out the property where his factory was located, which he had previously only rented.

This relatively short period of time was also one of experimentation in the bicycle, and Hendee had taken a keen interest in the various, not always successful, attempts to apply the principles of motorised transport to the conventional two-wheeler. Although many had tried to produce a workable prototype capable of mass production, the right formula seemed to remain tantalisingly out of reach. This didn't stop people trying though and the closest the early pioneers seemed to come were so-called 'pacing' machines, used for bicycle races.

This technique had developed on French velodromes and involved the use of a motorised bicycle designed to run ahead of a racing pack in order to create a slipstream and reduce the wind resistance they faced in order to allow them to truly test how fast they could go. Usually tandems, these machines were steered, and their speed controlled from, the front; while the second rider was typically an engineer whose job it was to keep the machine going. These early bikes were far from reliable, with many actually being overtaken by the impatient cyclists they were supposed to be helping. Breakdowns were a common occurrence and a stock of machines had to be kept on standby just in case.

Still, there seemed to be something there, even if exactly what that 'something' was remained unclear. In 1898 a number of these French machines were imported into the US by a professional rider called Kenneth Skinner, who trialled them in his native New York at the Madison Square Garden the following year. It was time for the second major actor in this tale to take the stage.

Carl Oscar Hedstrom was, as his name might suggest, of Swedish origin having been born in that country in 1871 and coming to the United States in 1880 when his family emigrated and came to Brooklyn. From an early age Oscar (as he preferred to be known once he'd arrived in America) showed a talent for engineering. After serving an apprenticeship in the manufacture of watchcases, he found employment in a range of small light engineering outfits around New York. Like Hendee, though, his real passion was for bicycles and he started to manufacture his own which he sold to professional racers.

In 1899 he obtained one of the French pacing machines imported by Kenneth Skinner and worked on it to improve its performance and reliability. Before too long he turned his hand to producing his own version which proved to be by some distance the most reliable on the circuit. It was this that caught the attention of George Hendee. In the autumn of 1900 the two got together and discussed their shared dream of producing a machine capable of mass production, leading Hedstrom to set up a workshop in the Worcester Cycle Company in Middletown, Connecticut.

The resulting prototype comprised a single-cylinder engine set in a conventional bicycle frame with a crankcase just above the chainwheel bracket, and the cylinder taking the place of the seat tube. Perhaps the bike's most remarkable feature was a two-section tank over the rear wheel, which came to be known as a 'camel back', although another contender was the shift away from the usual belt transmission to an all-chain drive.

Hedstrom was to be seen test-driving his new machine, painted deep blue and with nickel-plated small parts, around the countryside until he was happy to unveil it to the world. Hendee arranged a demonstration on Cross Hill Street in Springfield attended by various members of the press, at which the new motorised bike performed impressively, being stopped and re-started several times on the hill's notorious 19-degree slope. Hendee raised $20,000 on the back of the favourable publicity this short trip generated and Hedstrom began to produce his bike, although slowly at first with only six resulting from the rest of the year, two of which were sold.

Using what was now a well-tested formula, the bike was exhibited at track meetings and one was even shipped over to the UK to the Stanley Bicycle Show, where it again received favourable testimonials. By the end of 1902 143 bikes had been sold and the company had been incorporated as the Hendee Manufacturing Company, with George Hendee as the President and General Manager and Carl Hedstrom as the Chief Engineer and Designer. In an effort to encapsulate an 'all-American' association with their new product, Hendee and Hedstrom gave their bike the name 'Indian'.

Again demonstrating their flair for publicity, the pair entered their new Indian in a number of endurance trails and made sure that the bike received widespread coverage in the flourishing bicycling press. In 1903 Hedstrom set a new world record for a motorcycle of 56mph. The following year the manufacturing facilities in Springfield were expanded with the help of the sale of more shares and, in what must have been a defining moment, the trade name of the bicycles still being produced there was also changed to Indian. At the same time, the so-called 'Crimson Steed of Steel' colour scheme was introduced to help the product stand out from its otherwise mostly grey competitors, and the Indian won the Gold Medal for Mechanical Excellence at the St Louis Exposition.

In these early years the firm's two founding partners took a close personal involvement in the development of the business. Hendee devoted much of his energy to cultivating the dealer network which he knew from his bicycle days would be integral to any long-term strategy, whilst Hedstrom continued to innovate. The 1905 version of the bike saw the introduction of a sprung front fork to provide a better ride as well as the accelerator being operated from a twist-grip on the left-hand side of the handlebar and the magneto advance and retard being operated by a twist grip on the right-hand side. Sales of 586 in that year doubled to 1,181 the following year, and when a new twin-cylinder model was introduced the following year sales rose to 1,698.

A seal of approval of sorts was won for the Indian in 1907 when the New York Police Department placed their first ever motorcycle order with the company. Ostensibly it was to chase down runaway horses – a real problem at the time – a move which led the company to standardise the left-hand throttle control in order to allow officers to use their more usual right hand for other purposes including, it has been said, to use their firearm. This development was to have a significant impact on the Indian's popularity with Wall of Death riders later.

1907 was to prove significant in this history for two other reasons. First it marked the firm's transfer of facilities to new premises, also in Springfield, in order to keep up with increasing demand, with the plant in time earning the nickname 'The Wigwam'; and second because of growing interest in Indians in overseas markets. This was prompted in part by victory in the first Thousand Mile Reliability Trial held on public roads in England which was won by an Indian with a score which far out-paced its rivals.

The home market remained the company's main focus though, and Hendee worked hard to develop a sense of common ownership amongst the Indian community using ploys such as annual gatherings at dealerships known as

'Indian Days' and tours around the new 'Wigwam' plant. Loyalty was also inspired by the bike's both real and cultivated image of reliability, a major attraction to those outside the immediate enthusiast market. Roots laid down at this time have permeated the bike's legacy ever since, as we shall see.

Meanwhile, at the same time that the Reliability Trial was inaugurated in England the Isle of Man Tourist Trophy had been founded and Indians went on to take a clean sweep of the top three positions in 1911. Fast and reliable, and a flamboyant red colour too: was it any wonder that the Indian was cementing its position as the country's leading motorcycle? And not just in America. The bike's reputation in England spread throughout what was still the British Empire and dealerships were established as far afield as Australia and South Africa, as well as England itself. President Hendee made the journey across the Atlantic to sign the deal which gave the import rights to William H. Wells, with Hendee helping to joint finance a showroom in Great Portland Street, London.

Motorcycles were now beginning to replace bicycles in the public's imagination and board-track racing started to grow in popularity. Both 'official' and private Indians entered into these races, leading to the demolition of a number of records along the way. Where board tracks weren't available dirt tracks were used, typically at county fairs, which all added to the general sense that motorcycles were here to stay. By 1909 the firm was producing close to 5,000 machines, with law enforcement bodies now a significant customer. Encouraged by this, and the publicity that ensued from racing success, the firm embarked upon a major expansion of the Springfield plant in 1911, again financed by an expansion of the share capital.

However, despite outward appearances, soon all was not well in the Hendee camp. Despite counting production in the tens of thousands by this time tensions were beginning to appear between the shareholders, whose primary interest was in dividends, and Hendee and Hedstrom, whose interests lay beyond this. Hendee was still greatly involved in the publicity and racing side of things whilst Hedstrom was a stickler for quality. Profit per unit sold was low and, as soon became apparent, the constant issuing of share capital over the years meant that the firms' founders had lost control of 'their' company.

Boardroom disputes followed in 1913, a year when the company was to sell 32,000 bikes (around 40% of the domestic market, although 25% of production was exported). Hedstrom resigned, and left the motorcycle industry altogether, although he continued to exercise his talents with a new interest, one which he'd begun whilst with Hendee: aircraft engines. It was the end of an era, but not the end of the company; and it was at this time that the Wall of Death featured for the first time in the Indian story.

The occasion was a report in the company publication *Honest Injun* of three riders called Altona Edwards, George Botha and Will Wilson who were touring South Africa with what was called a vast 'wooden bowl' 45ft in circumference, 15ft high and banked to an angle of 75 degrees. The report cited Edwards as saying that they found Indians 'best suited for performance purposes, both on account of strength and speed.' He was also quoted as saying that he would ride no other machine but the Indian as he performed twelve to fourteen times a day and his life depended on the machine.

The same report suggested that Indians were also popular in Hollywood, especially in the production of what it called 'war plays'. Little did the report know quite how prescient this was, as within a year conflict had broken out in Europe and although the United States was not to join the fight for another three years the war had a radical impact on the Hendee company, not least because of the large proportion of sales which were exported. At the same time, the company found itself supplying a large number of machines (41,000) to the US Army, although this too led to boardroom disquiet as there was a dispute over the price the company charged for them. In the end this was to be the final straw for Hendee, who followed Hedstrom out of the door in 1916.

The war coincided with a downturn in demand for motorcycles, in the US at least, and the firm also experienced a series of labour disputes which did nothing to aid profitability. Despite continuing demand from overseas, where the company was now sending half its production, the company lost $1 million in 1922 and a new man, Frank Weschler, took the helm. A profit of $200,000 was returned in 1923 but by this time the company was facing severe competition from the motor industry, with a mass-produced car costing about to same as a large-capacity V-twin bike. That same year the company changed its name to The Indian Motocycle Company, with the loss of the 'r' in motorcycle deliberate.

By this time the era of economic protectionism was underway and this in turn led to a series of import tariffs. The 33% levy imposed by the UK government on motor vehicles forced the distributor there, Billy Wells, out of business within two months in 1925. 1926 saw the production of one of Indian's last factory racers, which utilised Scout fuel and oil tanks, a modified Scout-type frame with Powerplus front forks and scroll spring. These were to set records that would last for another ten years, reaching speeds up to 132mph at Daytona Beach.

Further boardroom battles saw Weschler leave in 1927 and the new regime looked for diversification opportunities. At the same time the Hoover administration started to impose levies on imported food from key Indian markets such as Australia and New Zealand, which in turn led to retaliatory import taxes from the governments of those countries. What had been a highly lucrative source of business dried up almost overnight.

Demoralisation set in amongst the workforce, who had largely supported Weschler and were less in favour of moving away from the traditional motorcycle market. Any profits made from the bikes seemed also to be 'invested' in new ventures, with the new board even dabbling in the production of a motorcar, a project which never came to fruition. At the same time although the company continued to experience racing success it found itself facing increasing competition on home soil from other manufacturers such as Harley Davidson, Henderson and Excelsior.

This was to turn out to be a low point for the company. It lost a large part of its reputation amongst its distributors, previously one of the company's greatest assets, as a result of supplying bikes with parts missing and, a year later, by only agreeing to supply bikes 'cash on delivery' as the financial squeeze tightened within the company. After further experiments in aircraft and outboard motor production a new president pulled in the horns and concentrated resources on motorcycle production exclusively. By 1932 the company was producing only three models which saw a stabilisation of the finances, although not enough to return to profit. The coming of the Great Depression made matters even worse, not only with regard to costs but also in releasing fleets of second-hand cars onto the market.

The coming of the Second World War in 1939 led to production concentrating on machines for military use, notably the 741, an adaption of the Indian Scout, with contracts placed by a number of allied forces. At the same time, parts of the Wigwam were converted to the production of materials for the war effort and after the war the Indian Motocycle Company struggled to regain its former momentum, albeit one which had been in decline for some years before. In 1945 it was consolidated into the Torque Engineering Company and subsequently divided between manufacturing, which went to the Atlas Corporation, and distribution, which was partitioned into The Indian Sales Corporation. These moves were not able to hold back what was beginning to look inevitable, however, and despite a re-introduction of the Chief model production came to a halt in 1953.

Since that time there have been various attempts to revive the Indian brand, but they seem to come and go like the seasons. Indian left a legacy, however, in an iconic marque, one that is still revered to this day by a certain breed of motorcycle enthusiast. Foremost amongst these are the men and women who risk their lives for a living and for whom the Indian isn't simply just another bike, but the bike of choice for everyone in their profession. They are Wall of Death riders and it is pertinent that we should now turn our attention to the history behind this particular feature of Indian folklore.

Above: An early postcard advertising the Iron Redskin.

Right: Indian's London base in Euston Road, with insets showing the Springfield works.

Clockwise from top left:

A proud owner of one of the earlier Indians, complete with flying helmet!

A postcard showing soldier W.H. Johnson on an Indian during the First World War.

A 1920s Indian Scout, originally Tornado Smith's trick bike, still in original condition.

The 1926 Speedway racer, one of the last factory racers.

SERIES II
Card 18

1941 Military
Scout

Model L
741 Military
Scout

Features
30.07 cu. in.
15 HP.

The U.S. Military used very few of the 741's when they discovered the Jeep, and most were sold to the allied countries during W.W.II.

Because of this, 741 Scouts are common in Britain, Australia and throughout Europe.

The 741 Military Scout shown is owned by Wayne Clarke of Castleton, NY.

MADE IN U.S.A.

"Old *Indians* Will Never Die"

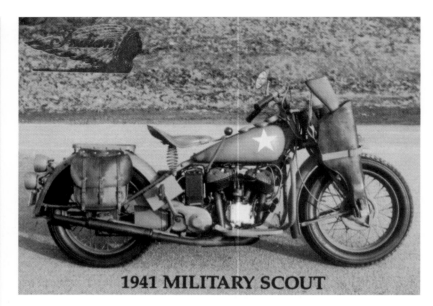

1941 MILITARY SCOUT

Above: The Military Scout as described on the back of a cigarette card.

Above right: A 1941 Military Scout as depicted on the same card.

Right: A nicely restored 741B in military trim.

Above: A rare 1910 racing Indian on the front of the show.

Above right: A typical rider and his Indian in the early 1920s. Note the wheel discs.

Right: Casual and debonair, dressed to kill but perhaps not to ride, around the 1930s.

My Indian

GODFREY'S LTD.
208
Great Portland St.
W.

Left: A pre-war advertising postcard for Indians.

Above: Taking the girlfriend for a spin in the (Indian) sidecar – note the union flags.

Below: A French velodrome pacing machine in the early years of the twentieth century.

CHAPTER 2

FROM CYCLES TO SILODROMES

The roots of the attraction that came to be known as the Wall of Death go deep and have already been hinted at in this narrative. Speed has always held a fascination to man, and it is perhaps natural that he has sought to find ways to enhance his ability to attain it. The bicycle was perfect for this purpose and in the early part of the twentieth century a primeval interest seemed to develop in seeing one human pit his strength and prowess against another in races using this new invention.

Typically, these took place on simple oval tracks, a format that would have been familiar to the ancient world and one that might be regarded as the 'purest' way to identify a worthy champion. It didn't take long, however, for new ways of exploiting the bicycle's potential to emerge, ones connected more to entertainment than sport. The oval track has its place, but by its very nature it is a large facility to keep going and not always conducive for spectators to appreciate the action taking place below them.

In the early 1900s the theatrical stage was the preferred medium for entertainment and it was here that showmen and impresarios saw an opportunity to showcase speed. The earliest known example of this was an invention patented in 1901 by an Australian called Charles Henry Jones, which involved a circular wooden track made up of a series of upright slats supported by legs on the outside, with the whole apparatus set up in a way to allow spectators to view what was going on inside through the gaps in the slats. Designed to be erected and taken down easily, Jones's 'Improved Course or Track for Cycling' was aimed specifically at the entertainment market and even highlighted 'music halls or other stages' in its patent application.

Within a year, Jones's invention was wowing audiences in the UK, with a review in *The Strand* magazine describing what was now being called the Jones-Hilliard Bicycle Sensation as a 'gigantic soup-plate with the edges shaved off and part of the front sliced out like a Wedgwood card-basket'. From this review we know that the bowl was 18ft in diameter with each slat 5ft long and that the gaps between them existed only at the front, where they were reduced to only 2in wide, with the back portion remaining flush all the way round to allow the cyclist to build up speed. This construction suggests that the 'sensation' was intended purely for stage use, rather than outdoor or fairground presentation.

The Jones-Hilliard Sensation can be seen as a precursor to the Wall of Death that was to follow, with a series of different stunts and the use of a 'spieler' to drum up trade from outside. Again, this tells us something about the show, in that it operated as a 'stand alone' attraction rather than an act in a wider variety show. The Sensation was only one example of the way things were going, however. Other variations included smaller constructions such as the 'Bowl of Death' (notable for introducing the suggestion of mortality) in which riders rode up to the lip of their bowl and performed feats which would also later enter the pantheon of Wall of Death stunts, such as riding side-saddle, standing up and even the removal of clothes, the latter a speciality of a rider called Charlie Jones. More compact and not requiring gaps on one side to allow the audience to see the action, these bowls were popular at outdoor venues such as fairs or even piers.

Speed had exerted its fascination and the public's appetite for it had been whetted. The invention of small petrol-powered engines offered up a whole new arena of possibilities, although it took a little while for this potential to be realised. By this time bicycle racing tended to take place on what were known as board tracks, some of which incorporated banking. Experiments had been taking place in France to spice up more conventional bicycle racing with the introduction of a motorised pace-setter bike designed to stretch the limits of human endurance by providing a slipstream thus reducing the wind resistance facing riders and allowing them to reach even greater speeds.

Although early versions of these machines were patchy in their effectiveness and reliability, their potential was clear to organisers and engineers alike, including, as has been mentioned, Oscar Hedstrom. By the second decade of the twentieth century this potential was beginning to be realised, although in the chase to achieve it safety was sacrificed in the pursuit of speed. Banks became ever higher and the bikes were stripped down to the bare essentials, a description which didn't include either brakes or clutches, with control exercised through the simple expedient of an engine cut out. Accidents were inevitable. Six spectators were fatally wounded in a crash at the Newark Motordrome, New Jersey, in 1912, the latest in a catalogue of disasters which forced the authorities to close down the track. This generated a domino effect across other states which effectively killed off board track racing, although oval dirt tracks remained.

As had happened with bicycles, an alternative means of demonstrating speed and entertaining the crowds with this new technology was required and it was at this point that history started to repeat itself with the exploits of one Erle Armstrong. A champion cyclist who had become interested in motorcycles – he worked as an engineer for an Indian dealership in Denver – Armstrong had moved into board track racing and was a factory rider for Hendee. As the tracks began to close down he turned his attention first to endurance racing, winning a 300-mile race in Tacoma, Washington, in record time, and then to a new form of attraction which he termed a 'Silodrome'.

Similar to the wooden bowls used by trick cyclists, Armstrong's Silodrome was so-called because it looked like a grain silo, sharing with these fixtures of the American countryside the distinction of having perfectly vertical sides, with the speeds obtainable on motorcycles making riding on a straight up and down surface possible. Again, like the bowls, these were made of wooden slats with gaps between them to allow spectators to view the action. The Silodrome was a hit straightaway and in his first year of operation Armstrong was asked to perform at the Panama-Pacific Exhibition in San Francisco where he performed not only alone, but also with his wife using a specially constructed tandem motorcycle.

Armstrong's notoriety was to be short-lived, however, as within a year he found himself working as part of the war effort, in charge of an Army motorcycle training school in Oklahoma before going on to run an Indian dealership after the war. Although Armstrong's claim to be the father of the modern Wall of Death may be a strong one, he wasn't alone in devising ways of using motorcycles in static displays. Mention has already been made of the Wilson/Edwards/Botha South African attraction which used Indians, and across the Atlantic British audiences had been entertained by two troupes known as the Tom Davis Trio and the Hall & Wilson Trio.

The Tom Davis Trio was particularly notable for their act which involved riding round a circular wooden saucer-shaped track which could be raised into the air so that the riders seemed to defy gravity as they spun round their suspended track which, in an echo of the Jones-Hilliard Sensation, had a diameter of 18ft and a height of only 5ft, leaving very little margin for error. As the appetite for seemingly frivolous entertainment seemed to evaporate in Europe in the face of the stark reality of war, Davis went on to tour the US and Australia with his troupe, which used Levis as their bike of choice.

It was to be a decade before anything similar to the pre-war motorcycle entertainments were to be seen again in the UK, and even then it was only as a curiosity, with some evidence surviving that Globes of Death, large mesh spheres which bikes went round inside, were travelling the countryside at this time. A depressed economy seemed only to compound a mood that seemed to suggest that the reckless risking of life simply wasn't appropriate after so many young men had lost theirs fighting in the trenches for King and Country. It was in an effort to shake off this despondency that the British Empire Exhibition was organised in 1924, and it was at this event that a 'Death Ring' appeared, a throwback to the likes of Tom Davis before the war.

The attraction was described as 'a cup-shaped steel cage [in which] a motor cyclist, and sometimes three, ride around the top of the track in a horizontal position and parallel to the ground.' The official programme for the exhibition gives no clues as to who the riders were, but it seems likely that they emanated from abroad. It is known that Walls of Death were enjoying success in South Africa, at that time still a British Dominion and therefore likely to feature in the exhibition, although documentary evidence tends to suggest that this was more towards the latter part of the decade, leaving riders from the United States more likely candidates.

Silodromes had continued in operation across the Atlantic throughout the hostilities, with the Parker Amusement Company owning a number of touring versions. At this time the formula tended to focus on two riders racing each other round the inside of the Wall, but once crowds got used to the idea of bikes seemingly sticking to the side of the Wall without falling this didn't seem to be enough. County fairs and carnivals, the most promising locations for a Wall, demanded something more, and it fell to the Purtle Brothers, led by Earl Purtle, to develop it. Not only did they innovate with the drome itself, introducing a safety cable round the top of the Wall and reinforcing cables around the outside to make the structure more stable, but they also experimented with the show.

Earl taught himself a repertoire of tricks such as riding side-saddle and even introduced cars and lions to the Wall and learned that the 'oohs and aahs' of the crowd inside the drome, combined with the sound of the bikes themselves, would rapidly draw a crowd. It was then the job of the 'spieler' to convert this crowd into paying customers. In the 1920s the Purtles owned two Walls, one permanent one at Palisades Park, New Jersey, and another on the road with the Cetlin-Wilson Carnival. The Palisades Park Wall was larger than those seen before the war at 33ft in diameter and 14½ft high, further confirmation that the Purtles were not afraid to try out new ideas.

Despite the appearance of the 'Death Ring' at the British Empire Exhibition it seemed that the British appetite for Walls had yet to be really stimulated. Here, and generally in Europe, the tendency had been for motorcycle acts to stay with the idea of operating within a steel cage, more likely to be saucer shaped than vertical, with customers looking at rather than down on the act. Again, there is more evidence of touring Globes of Death than Walls of Death in Europe at this time, with France taking the lead.

Meanwhile, performers in America were, if anything, suffering from too much competition. It is difficult, perhaps, in these days of mass communication to imagine how the two continents could develop their own styles of entertainment so completely separately, but this appears to have been the case. It took the need to find fresh audiences for one or two pioneering American troupes to take the large step of packing their Walls onto a ship and sending them 'over the pond' to see how they fared amongst a fresh audience.

This was no one-off, with at least two proprietors sending Walls over in the late 1920s: The American Amusement Company and the Silodrome Company. These two arrived at much the same time, a fact that has led to some dispute over the years as to who was first, but what we do know is that the American Amusement Company advertised for local riders to its 'Wizards of the Wall' attraction, suggesting that their intention was less to offer a package of entertainment rather than the concept, possibly with the aim of making their money through licences or through the sale of the actual Walls themselves.

One of the first to answer the call was a Sheffield-based former speedway rider called Billy Bellhouse or 'Cyclone Billy', who became so proficient he went on to tour Europe and North Africa with the Wall. The first written record of a Wall in the UK was in the fairground journal *World's Fair* in June 1929 where six riders were said to be performing, two of whom were South African, with the Wall itself owned by a third company, Motor Silodromes Pty

(Ltd). This does not mean it was the first Wall in the UK, however, and over the years a number of different claims have been made for this crown, with a Wall in Belle Vue, Manchester, the year before often cited.

What seems most likely is that from a position of no Walls at all, the UK was suddenly swamped with them, with other claimants for one of the earliest being the one at Pleasureland in Ramsgate, also owned by Silodromes Pty (although it was operated by Auto-Rides Ltd), and one in Kelvin Hall in Glasgow the same year. Any sense of nationalism in favour of the European tradition of steel-mesh globes seemed to give way to the attractions of the Wall.

In a pattern that may be familiar to modern sensibilities, it seems that the European version was more dangerous and more technically challenging, but the American attraction was more of a spectacle, and this was what drew the crowds. In another twist, it was also easier to process Wall crowds more quickly using the formula pioneered by the Purtle brothers, making the Wall a more profitable proposition. Proprietors were happy, the public were fascinated and riders seemed to be available – the scene was set for the Wall of Death to take European audiences by storm.

Of these three factors the most surprising perhaps was the availability of riders. The format of a Wall of Death show was by this time fairly well set and whilst it may not have been as technically demanding as being a Globe rider it did still require no little talent – and experience. Whilst it is possible for a rider with sufficient skill and nerve to learn to go round a Wall fairly quickly it takes much longer to gain the proficiency to stunt ride, usually around a year, whereas sheer recklessness, combined with a good dash of enthusiasm, in an age not governed by Health & Safety regulations, would have been enough to see them 'straight-riding' on the Wall within a week or two.

Another explanation may have been the suppressed demand for something new, not only amongst the public but also amongst the riders, who now represented a new generation from those who had fallen in the Great War. Dirt track and speedway racing provided a pool of skilled riders who might perhaps have been ready to take on a new challenge, one which combined technical difficulty with the thrill of the new, with the added extra of a patina of glamour coming as it did from over the Atlantic. Another explanation might be that Walls may already have existed in the UK, but had gone unrecorded; although given the speed with which they gathered publicity subsequently this seems unlikely.

As an example of this the two popular newspapers the *Daily Mail* and the *Daily Express* both carried features on the Wall in 1930, with the former calling it 'the biggest thrill of all', whilst the latter called it 'an astonishing exhibition of nerve and dare-devilry'. Both these reports were on the same

Jones's Improved Course or Track for Cycling is a construction which is designed for use in cycle races or performances, on music hall and other stages and places of public amusement and in other places of limited area. It can be readily erected and removed as required and, being partly open or with interstices between the whole or a portion of the floor of the track so as to enable the spectators to see through it, is especially adapted for the above purposes.

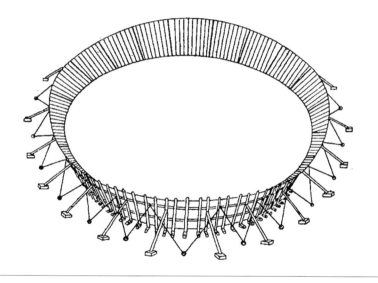

Wall, one being ridden by Lou 'Suicide' Cody, who was also known as 'Curly', alongside Winnie Souter, a teenage female rider who rode as 'Fearless Wyn'.

In this one example we can see a number of the traits that would subsequently characterise the Wall. Firstly, the involvement of a woman rider, which in itself was a comment on the changing status of women in society at the time, with universal female suffrage for example only coming about in 1928. Women riders rapidly became a feature of the Wall, a tradition that is maintained to this day, with their presence seeming to attract publicity. This in turn represents another feature of Wall riding: its understanding of the importance of showmanship and using this to pull in the public. Another trait is the use of hyperbole to exaggerate the riders' feats. A poster advertising the show, which took place at the Palace Gardens in New Brighton, suggested that the riders travelled at speeds of between 60-100mph, where 30-40mph would have been more accurate.

At the time Winnie was only 15 and her story demonstrates not only the speed with which riders came to the Wall but also how they got there. She learned how to ride from a pair of Canadian brothers called the Restalls, part of the influx of North American riders who had come to these shores and who understood the 'pulling power' of a woman rider. After a season riding alongside her sister Gladys and another female rider called June as the 'Wizards of the Wall' troupe in Scarborough the year before (another indication of the speed with which the Wall had infused itself into the UK entertainment scene), Winnie took up an offer to ride in New Brighton and never looked back. During the season her act attracted luminaries such as the Prince of Wales, Ramsey MacDonald and speed aces such as Sir Henry Segrave. Winnie's story therefore confirms that there were Walls around in 1929, but that it took a woman rider to make them really newsworthy!

In the meantime, American riders continued to tour the UK and Europe, with examples including Fearless Egbert and Speedy Williams, the latter a black rider who is usually credited with being the first to introduce lions on the Wall to the UK. A third American rider was Bob Carew, who started in the UK and, perhaps mindful of the proliferation of Walls there, went on to tour Europe starting in Holland and ending up in Russia, where he sold his Wall in 1938. Although not a major player on the UK scene, Carew did make a significant contribution to this book's story as it was he who introduced the Indian motorcycle not only to Wall audiences, but to their riders also. From that time on the Indian became the bike of choice for all Wall riders, so it is pertinent that we now turn our attention to why it became such as vital part of any Wall show.

THE WORLD'S FAMOUS **TOM DAVIES TRIO** ON THEIR LEVIS'S

Above: Boardtrack racing at the Milwaukee Motordrome, 1913.

Below: The Tom Davis Trio on their Levis's.

Above: Bring the Ladies!

Below: Spectators stand on the outside in this early form of the Wall.

Opposite page top: A description of the Patent for Jones Improved Track for Cycling.

Opposite page bottom: A rather faded but rare image of a Russian pacesetter and cyclist from *c.*1905.

APPEARING AT

KURSAAL   -   Southend-on-Sea

SILODROMES (PTY.) LTD.

present

For the first time in Europe, after Touring the World, America's latest and greatest
of all thrillers

THE WALL
OF DEATH

A Silodrome built at an angle of 90 degrees has been conquered.   Six of the
World's most daring and dare-devil Motor Cyclists, including

CAPT. BOB PERRY, CYCLONE JACK
CODY and PLUCKY JENNIE PERRY

ride on an absolutely Perpendicular Wall, defying death, doing trick, acrobatic, and
stunt riding, crossing and recrossing each other, and breaking all the laws of gravity.
Their daring, skill, courage and cleverness will brace every nerve in your system,
and give you the thrill of your life.

CAPT. MALCOLM CAMPBELL

who was recently in South Africa with his Blue Bird Car trying to break Major Sir Henry
Segrave's record, visited The Wall of Death and said,

"I HAVE NEVER SEEN ITS EQUAL IN ALL MY LIFE"

Johannesburg Sunda
April 14th, 1929,

" No wonder we cheered
when these intrepid mo
once more reached ter

Clockwise from top left:
Bridson-Greene's US Silodrome featuring 'Cyclone' Woods and 'Flying Hat'
Clayton.

Poster advertising what may have been the first Wall of Death in the UK.

One of the very first UK Walls featuring The Death Riders, Manchester Belle Vue.

Top: Stratford Mop 1930.

Above left: Hazel Russell and Speedy Bauer at Olympia 1929-30 season.

Above right: A rare example of bikes going the opposite way round at the same time.

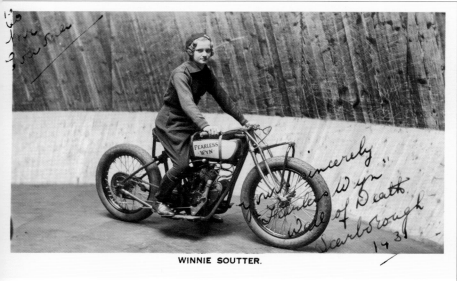

Top left: The Todd Brothers at Merrie England 1932 demonstrating the rare art of roller-skating on the Wall.

Top right: Speedy Curly Lee, his brother Billy Lee and Miss Ray James.

Above left: 'Fearless' Wyn Souter, Scarborough 1931.

Above right: Speedy Jack Rooney performing in Holland 1937.

Above: Tom Grave with his stage act, flying the revolving wheel.

Above right: The forerunner of the Wall of Death as a circus act.

Above left: Cyclone Danny, complete with tank pad.

Above right: Diagonal boards to give extra strength.

Left: The Drome of Death – sitting sideways without a tank pad.

CHAPTER 3

YOU CAN'T WEAR OUT AN INDIAN SCOUT

An integral part of a Wall of Death performance takes place on the bally or front of the show, where a spieler will stand up and exercise his skills of showmanship to whip up a crowd of potential 'punters' to the next show. An essential component of these skills is his well-rehearsed sales pitch, which he has to air hundreds of times a day but which has to sound fresh and convincing each time. The spieler's job is a specific one: he has to draw a crowd of people towards him like iron filings to a magnet and then choose his moment to play his ace card.

Having intrigued his audience with tales of seemingly impossible feats he gives a discrete nod to his colleague sitting on an Indian Scout resting on a set of rollers and all of a sudden the air is filled with a combination of exhaust fumes and noise as the rider fires up his bike and begins to demonstrate some of those self-same feats – standing up, standing on the saddle, sitting side-saddle and even sitting backwards, all the time maintaining control of the bike on the rollers as it swings to and fro, constantly threatening to topple over as it wobbles, seemingly on the edge of control.

At this point the first part of the spieler's work is done. His pitch has been vindicated; he's a man who can be trusted. It seems that the feats he has been describing are indeed possible and the obvious question that now joins the noise and exhaust fumes in the air over the crowd is this: 'If that looks spectacular, how much more extraordinary will it be to see them performed on the side of a vertical wall?'. From this point the spieler moves on to complete his work by showing the crowd where they need to go to pay to witness the apparent miracle he has been describing, what's known in the trade as 'turning the tip'.

Almost without exception the bike the punters will have been watching will have been an old Indian. Looking like an antique and held together with bits of wire and insulating tape, it appears an unlikely candidate for the demanding show described by the spieler, and part of the attraction to the paying public may well be seeing whether it is up to the task. Ask any Wall rider the two questions they are asked most often and they will almost certainly reply 'Do you ever fall off?' and 'Do you ever hurt yourself?' The answers to these are pretty straightforward – an emphatic 'Yes!' on both counts. There is a third question though, the answer to which is more complex, and that question is 'Why do you use old Indian motorcycles?'

The aim of this chapter is to answer that question, and the best place to start is by being clear about exactly which type of Indian Wall riders prefer. The bike of choice is the 1920s 600cc Scout. These are often confused with the 101 Scout which has sloping foot boards and a longer wheelbase of $57^{1}/_{8}$in, compared to $54^{1}/_{2}$in on the Scout. Some even confuse these with Indian Chiefs.

This is not to say that tricks and stunts cannot be performed on any other make or type of motorcycle. The difference is that if you make your living out of riding a Wall of Death, and indeed if your health and well-being is largely dependent upon your choice of bike, it is inevitable that you will want to use the best machine available for the task, whatever it may look like! The legendary riders Tornado Smith and Yvonne Stagg for example both performed at Southend riding BSA Rigid 500cc A7s, although they confessed to prefer riding Indian Scouts. In India, Iran and Thailand little 125cc two-stroke machines are also used, although walls in the Far East are usually home-built out of pallet wood and have a smaller diameter. In these situations it may be more a case of using what is available rather than what might be best.

Previous chapters have shown how the Indian Motocycle Company had achieved a leading place in the global marketplace by manufacturing one of the fastest, best handling and most reliable motorcycles in the world. The company's confidence in its product was summed up in the advertising slogan it used in the 1920s: 'You Can't Wear Out an Indian Scout', a claim which was founded on the fact that the materials used to manufacture the machines, especially the steel, were of the highest quality available in America at the time. Given the demands placed upon the bikes used by Wall of Death riders this acted as a good reason to choose the Indian, but the real reasons for making them the bike of choice are much more complex than that, with many of the bike's features all coming together to favour their use on the Wall.

Starting with the frame itself, which is rigid (that is to say there is no rear suspension), this has duplex front-down tubes – an unusual feature in the 1920s when the bikes were made – which are brazed into a cast-steel headstock which has strengthening gussets. Engine mounts and rear wheel lugs are also cast steel. Perhaps the most striking thing about the frame is its curved design, upholding the growing Art Deco-type appearance which was coming into vogue at the time and gave the bike a striking appearance, a combination of looking the part and being able to act the part adding to the bike's attraction.

The twin top tubes on the Indian provide a void for the flat-topped petrol tank with a compartment at the front for the engine oil which is fed through a copper pipe down to the total loss oil pump mounted on the timing cover. There is also a hand-operated plunger pump in the tank for supplying an extra shot of oil straight into the nearside crankcase if needed when riding at speed or climbing a steep hill, another feature which made the bike useful for Wall riding. Originally a fuel valve was located on the underside of the tank operated by a rod which passed through the petrol tank. Nowadays a standard fuel tap is usually used to replace the valve. A contributing factor to the suitability of these bikes for trick riding is the trailing link front forks, set at an angle of 60 degrees. Although only allowing limited travel of about 2in in all, they are adequate for Wall use.

The front leaf spring on the Indian is something Wall riders particularly value as it provides a platform on which to place the foot when moving forward over the handlebars. The suspension struts connecting the spring to the fork links vary in design and shape, being adapted to accommodate the front fender on road-going versions. As mentioned earlier, no two Indians handle the same on the Wall. For instance, if the gap between the front wheel and the down tube of the frame is two fingers in width the bike is great for performing steep dips whilst a gap of three fingers makes for a better trick bike.

The handlebars incorporate the top yoke and are held in place with a domed nut on the fork stem. This nut is also used to lock the steering head top bearing. Handlebars vary in shape and size, with some riders preferring them narrow and straight and others wide and curving back, with the way a rider performs tricks often proving to be a determining factor. Unlike most English motorcycles, the throttle and ignition advance and retard control wires run inside the handlebars. This is ideal for trick riding as the riders can't get caught in the cables when sitting on the handlebars or steering the bike with their feet – a key consideration when circling round the Wall at 30mph! Also, unlike all other makes of motorcycles, the accelerator control twist grip is on the left-hand side, going back to the days when the New York Police needed their right hand free for shooting gangsters. The Indian factory even made a Scout 45 Police Special (745cc), which was faster than a Chief.

A theme is already emerging here of riders adapting the Indian to suit their own particular foibles, riding style or their personal repertoire of tricks, and a good example of this is the saddle, a critical feature if you are going to spend most of your waking day astride the bike. Most of the saddles fitted these days have been sourced from ex-Army 741b Indians or Harley 45s, whilst some modern machines use modern fibreglass replacements. As long as the base is not rusted away these can be padded with new felt and recovered in black or brown leather, some even having tassels hanging down the back.

The original springs that supported the saddle usually have to be replaced with strong brackets, as when on the Wall a rider's weight with the added G-force forces causes the springs to compress right down. All these brackets seem to vary and this is a useful feature for bike historians as looking closely at them helps identify different machines from the past. A rear fender is often fitted these days and offers some protection to the rider's derrière should he (or she) slide off the rear of the machine whilst sitting backwards. Many feel that this also improves the look of a bike.

Now we come to the wheels. The bearings in the front and rear hubs were originally cup and cone with loose ball-bearings, although nowadays the hubs are modified to fit tapered roller-bearing races giving a great improvement. Originally the rims were shaped for 26 x 300 beaded-edge tyres, although most of these got replaced in the 1950s with WM2 or WM3 well-based chrome rims. Some people made the mistake of using spokes of too heavy a gauge which are prone to snapping when going on and off the Wall because they don't flex enough.

Brakes are not a priority for Wall of Death machines, as the rider does not have to apply them whilst on the Wall. A rear brake is, however, handy when the rider finishes his act and needs to come to a halt quickly in the centre of the floor ready to commence the next act, as every minute counts when there is a queue at the cash box. Front brakes were not fitted to Scouts, the rear brakes being of the internal drum and external band type to comply with the law, so that the bike had two independent braking systems.

Tyres are possibly the most crucial component on a trick bike. Speaking personally, the authors have found that a 3.50 x 19 ribbed tyre on the rear and a 3.25 x 19 ribbed tyre on the front, both inflated to a pressure of 39psi, works best although the actual pressures will vary a little from rider to rider. What every rider will agree on, however, is that trick bikes handle best when the tyres are worn in. To speed this process up the bike can be run up on the rollers at the front of the show and the edges cut down with a Surform rasp, but even then it pays to ride very carefully on new tyres, a lesson many a rider has learned the hard way! The friction of the rubber on the wooden wall combined with centrifugal force is what makes the show possible and periodically a prudent rider will check his tyres and wipe them over with a petrol soaked rag to remove any oil and dust which may build up on a dusty 'ground'.

When riding on old original walls dating back to the 1920s a part of the early morning checks each day will be an inspection of the interior surface of the Wall for protruding nail heads. When spotted these have to be punched back in as sharp nail heads tend to cut in to the tyres and will cause a puncture. If the rider should sustain a blow-out whilst trick riding, especially if sitting on the handlebars or facing backwards, he will inevitably fall – and this goes some way to providing the answer to the first two questions a punter will ask.

The positioning of the 42-degree V-twin engine gives the Indian a particularly low centre of gravity, which makes it ideal for trick riding. With a cylinder bore of 2¾in and a stroke of $3^{1}/_{16}$in, giving the Scout a cubic capacity of 600cc or 37 cubic inches. The engine was rated at 10hp. On the early models the cylinder barrel and head were cast as one piece with screw caps over the inlet and exhaust valves giving access to replace or grind in the valves. The size of the sparking plugs is 18mm on all models, with Indian even marketing their own.

The magneto is located on a platform cast into the front of the crankcase, and the Scouts came with either Bosch, Splitdorf, Dixie or Aero 42-degree magnetos. When these machines left the factory they were fitted with Schebler carburettors, but the best carburettor to use on a Wall Indian is made by Linkert, as fitted to the Military 741B. These run well with this set up and spares are easily available, still wrapped in WD waxed paper. The butterfly valve in the throat has to be operated by a push-and-pull piano wire connected to the left-hand twist grip. There are two adjusting screws, main jet and pilot jet, and final adjustments are best made whilst riding round the Wall as they are accessible using the left hand.

Exhaust pipes are an optional extra on a wall bike as the louder they go, the better the show! The crisp bark from the V-twin adds to the atmosphere of the show. When riders perform on silenced machines, however good their trick riding is it seems as if they are lacking something. If exhaust pipes are omitted altogether the flames from the exhaust port will burn the riders boots, which is both expensive and uncomfortable. Ideally, short, chrome-plated stubs about 6in long fixed to the lower frame rails work, look and sound the best.

A three-speed, hand-change gearbox is attached to the rear of the crankcases. The gear lever is located on the top of the right-hand side of the gearbox as these machines were designed to be hand change. However, when trick riding an Indian, second gear is selected by hand before pulling away, then when on the banking track the rider will change up by kicking the gear lever down into third gear with his or her right foot without using the clutch. The primary drive is by a train of helical gears running in an oil bath. The primary case also houses a multi-plate clutch which is operated by a foot pedal above the left-hand foot board. The final drive chain sprocket best suited for trick riding has seventeen teeth, equal to sidecar gearing on the road. Rear chain guards are dispensed with for wall riding.

The kick-starter fits on a spigot located on the right side of the frame's down tube, and on the road version a coil return spring is fitted and the kick-start is retained by a circlip. When wall riding, the kick-start is removed after the engine is started, as if it was retained the G-force would cause it to hang down whilst on the Wall. Indian fitted the kick-starter on the right-hand side as in America the sidecar, if fitted, was on the left-hand side of the machine.

Various modifications have evolved over the years to facilitate trick riding on an Indian Scout. Apart from removing the mudguards, dynamo and lighting equipment, the battery covers, toolboxes, horn, chain guard, silencer, carrier and both front and rear stands are dispensed with. Tank pads are made up out of thick felt, covered with leather secured with a leather strap. These make moving forward to sit side-saddle more comfortable – something that needs to be taken into account when performing twenty or thirty shows a day.

One of the reasons why the Scout is so good for trick riding is that the saddle and the top of the petrol tank are on the same plane, meaning the rider can move forward and back into the saddle easily. The left-hand foot board has a piece of angle iron attached to the outer edge. This is essential as when standing or sitting on the tank with your right foot on the front spring, it enables the rider to wobble and steer the machine using the outside of the left boot and the inside of the left thigh.

No two Indians feel the same on the wall; some riders like a bike to pull up the wall, others for it to steer straight, though it depends to some extent upon what tricks are in a rider's repertoire. For instance, when standing on the side of the machine with your left foot on the foot board and the right foot between the back wheel and the frame down tube, looking up at the audience, the bike has to pull up the wall. The technique used to make the bike pull up the wall is to remove the front wheel, making sure a note is made of the number of washers on the top right and left bottom side of the wheel spindle. The gap between the front fork legs is measured, then with a block of wood placed against the inside of the top fork leg the block is struck with a sledgehammer, which should bend the leg out about ¼in. The block is then put against the outside of the bottom leg and struck until the gap between the fork legs is the same as at the beginning. Having refitted the wheel the bike is taken up on the wall to assess how it handles 'no hands'. Should it need fine adjustment to pull up some more, the wheel is removed and a washer taken out from the top side and fitted on the wheel spindle's bottom side, moving the wheel over a small amount.

The other modification, made from a piece of old hacksaw blade, is an ignition cut-out button. A hacksaw blade is snapped off about 3in from the end, the teeth ground off, and a length of electrical wire connected by threading it through the hole. Insulation tape is wound round the handlebars about 3in from the right-hand twist grip, and the hacksaw blade is placed on top, making sure no part of the blade or wire touches the bars. This is secured with more insulating tape, leaving about an inch protruding which the rider presses with his or her thumb to make the engine backfire, adding to the ambience of the show.

Taken together all these features explain why the 1920s Indian Scout is the ideal motorcycle for the Wall of Death. In the words of the world's most successful Indian motorcycle dealer, Sammy Pierce:

> *You can't wear out an Indian Scout,*
> *or its brother the Indian Chief.*
> *They're built like rocks to stand hard knocks,*
> *it's the Harleys that cause the grief.*

Neil Calladine spieling while Kerry Cameron performs a bally for the Ken Fox Troupe 2006.

Powerplant of a 1925 Indian Scout. Note original Schebler carburettor and dynamo driven off the primary drive.

Ken Fox's trick bike, a 1925 Sports Scout, showing the topside.

Ken Fox's trick bike from another angle, showing the bottom side.

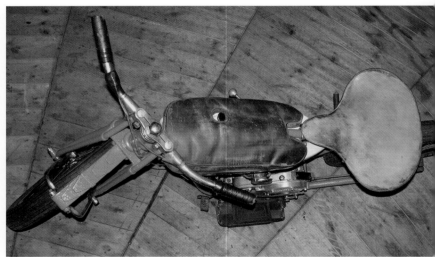

Above: Leaf spring and front forks of a Wall bike.

Above right: Powerplant as used on the Wall of Death. Note no dynamo and Linkert carburettor.

Below right: View from above showing tank pad, cut-out switch and fairly straight handlebars

Note straight struts connecting leaf spring to the fork links.

Note curved struts to give clearance for a mudguard.

Above left: Set up for road use, showing trailing link and front brake.

Above right: Band brake-type rear-brake assembly. When new this would have had an additional internal expanding brake also operating in this drum.

Below left: Final drive sprocket on band brake hub.

Below right: Final drive sprocket and brake drum fitted on the top side – the most common type of rear brake.

Above left: Timing side of engine. Note flat footboards, rear foot brake lever, gear change lever and total loss oil pump.

Above right: An example of showman's bodge – a BSA front wheel and an improvised tank under the saddle at the back.

Right: A 101 Sports Scout with sloping foot board, a shortened frame and horizontally mounted engine bolts – taken together these made this bike unsuitable for the Wall of Death. Note the broken piston skirt.

Three-speed gearbox bolts directly on the crankcase.

Carburettor spares pack still in its waxed paper.

A dismantled left-hand twist-grip assembly.

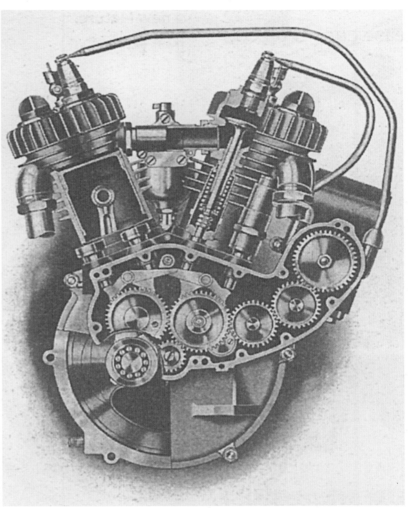

A cutaway diagram of an Indian Scout engine.

A 1920 Indian Scout primary drive. Inside a cast aluminium housing a set of three helical gears were set in an oil bath.

Above left: A 101 Scout being ridden on a German Wall. Note the leather strap on front forks (in case the leaf spring breaks) and semi-road trim.

Above right: The same bike as it is now in a museum in Germany.

Left: A restored 101 Scout in road trim.

Ken Fox banging the front forks over so that the bike pulls up the Wall, assisted by his son Alex.

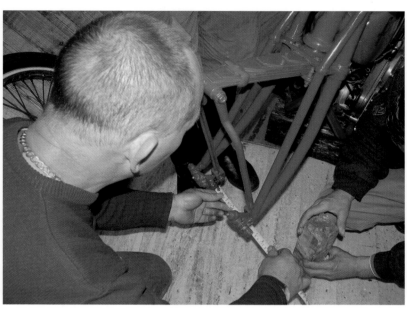

Ken Fox measuring the distance between the fork legs.

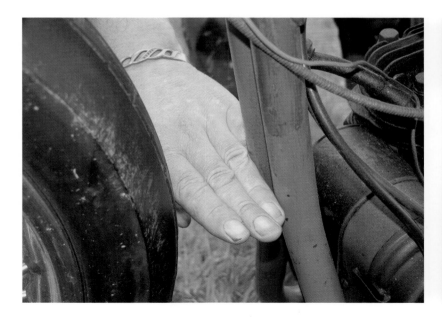

The finger test.

A new take on the Indian logo.

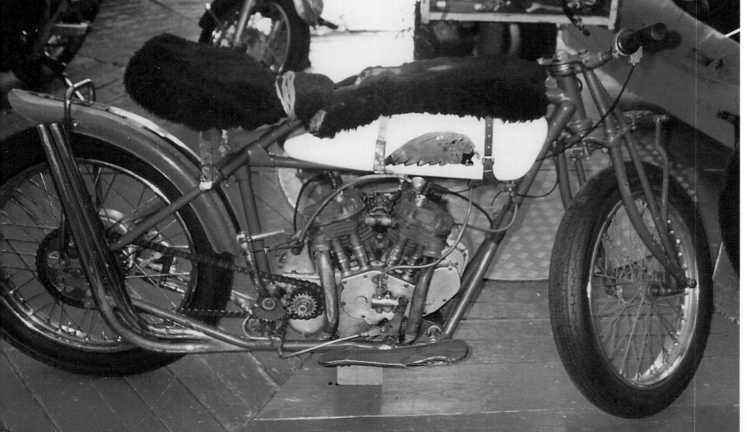

Above left: This bike has been hand-painted at the beginning of every season and that's about all the attention its had, yet someone is still making a living riding it.

Above right: An Indian power plant.

Left: Note upswept exhaust.

CHAPTER 4

THE HEYDAY OF THE WALL

It may have taken a while for the Wall of Death to evolve into the attraction we know today, but once it had taken shape both riders and proprietors wasted no time in making it a phenomenon. A formula had been created, one which covered not only the nature of the attraction but its content and how to make money from it. Such was the robustness of this formula that it has hardly changed over the last eighty years.

Perhaps the secret of this success has been simplicity, not only in concept but also in execution. The idea of men (and women) riding motorcycles perpendicular to a straight surface seems to defy nature, and it is this which initially grabs the interest of a potential customer. After that it is simply a case of enticing that same customer to part with his or her money by demonstrating, on a set of rollers outside the wall, a series of tricks and stunts that will that quite literally have to be seen to be believed. Meanwhile, from inside the wall can be heard the sounds not only of the bikes performing the show but also the cries and shouts from the crowd watching it.

It is here that a key part of the formula lies: a current show and a gathering crowd in order to help to generate the next one. The Wall's structure is designed to get people in and out quickly, with the minimum of fuss, on a good day creating a conveyor belt of action and paying customers, with each member of the team knowing exactly what his or her role is and, through repetition, perfecting it to maximum efficiency.

By the early 1930s this was an enticing prospect for fairground owners keen to offer their entertainment-hungry audiences something new, a move away from rides towards attractions which customers paid to witness rather than experience directly. Big circuses were a common feature around Christmas in major cities at this time, with most having an indoor funfair and Wall of Death attached to them. At other times of the year, travelling funfairs were also a popular form of diversion for the working classes, with attractions such as boxing booths, parading shows and freak shows all vying with one another for the customer's small change at gatherings such as the Stratford Mop, which could trace its antecedents back for centuries. Walls of Death, along with Globes of Death, were a natural addition to this roster, with some fairs accommodating more than one Wall. Likewise, permanent amusement parks, typically in seaside locations such as Margate, Ramsgate, Barry, Southend and naturally Blackpool followed a similar model, as did Manchester Belle Vue away from the sea.

Such was the universality of the attraction of the Wall that its appeal stretched beyond the UK. Mainland Europe was also quick to latch onto its appeal, with the Munich Oktoberfest and the Hamburg Dom both featuring a number of Walls, as well as locations in France and the Low Countries. Walls also continued to be popular in other parts of the British Empire, notably South Africa and Australia, although the home of the Wall, and the Indian, remained the United States, where Silodromes were still a popular feature of county shows.

Riders might be attracted to work for a particular showman or to 'freelance', or more often a mix of the two, and a good example of this was the husband and wife team Cyclone Chris and Daredevil Ena Goosen, he being a South African by birth and Ena originally a native of Whitley Bay, Durham. As an example of the show's international appeal the couple enjoyed a successful tour of Lebanon, Syria and Palestine over eighteen mouths from 1934-5, during which they rode not only bikes on their Wall but drove an Austrian-made car, returning to tour not only in Ireland and Scotland, riding on their own Wall, but also at Barry's show in Portrush.

In the days before every home had a television in the front room live entertainment was central to most people's lives, whether this be at the weekends or on their holidays. In the 1930s motorcycles seemed to speak of modernity and were the transport of choice for the working man. As a result most understood what it took to ride a bike – its weight, how it handled, the speeds it could reach and what it felt like to travel at those speeds – and as such most could appreciate the skills the Wall of Death demonstrated. This also meant, of course, that there wasn't a shortage of young men prepared to try to become Wall riders themselves, which was just as well as by the middle of the decade there were as many as fifty Walls either touring or part of a static funfair in the UK alone.

Despite the apparent dangers, there were a number of attractions to becoming a Wall of Death rider. With unemployment numbers rising the apparent prospect of a carefree life, ready access to female company and a reasonable wage, to say nothing of the glamour and, if you were really successful, a fair amount of fame, must have been enticing to many a young man. In reality, many came forward but the number who stuck at it enough to become really proficient was much smaller. A belief that they could replicate the exploits of the riders on the Wall, combined perhaps with a suspicion that there was some trickery involved which made it look harder than it in fact was, must have been alluring. At the same time, proprietors were also happy to feed this perception by appearing to be willing to take on local riders as the prospect of 'one of their own' seemed to pull in the crowds. In reality, those same proprietors knew that few would put in the graft required to become a good trick rider and rare was the novice who lasted more than a season.

As Walls began to grip the public's imagination a distinction grew up between owners, owner-proprietors and riders with their own Walls. By some distance the most prolific owner was Billy Butlin, who had seen the potential of the attraction early on and attempted to secure a near-monopoly of the production from the UK's main producer of Walls of Death, the amusement ride manufacturers Orton & Spooner. Over time, Butlin probably bought around twenty Walls from the company, making it difficult for others to break their way in during the early days of the attraction. Butlin's business model was to own the Wall and rent it out to presenters such as Marshalls or Greens, keeping back an increasing proportion over time for his burgeoning portfolio of holiday camps. Another following a similar model was the established fairground operator Pat Collins.

Owner-proprietors also tended to own more than one Wall and, like the presenters, who were effectively renting their Walls, they would hire in riders, who as a consequence would tend to follow the highest offer. Riders with their own Walls, on the other hand, had more at stake and had to invest not only in their physical asset but also their own skills, learning new tricks and seeking to come up with innovations to keep themselves one step ahead of the competition.

Such was the demand, however, that other established fairground families managed to acquire their own Walls and by the early 1930s there were dozens of Walls on the road and in static parks in the UK, with the show enjoying equal popularity in other parts of the globe ranging from Australia and South Africa through to the home of the show, the US. Meeting this demand meant getting an adequate supply of riders, and although this didn't seem to be much of a problem, a bigger issue was supplying these riders with bikes. As we have seen, the bike of choice was the Indian Scout, and although these had been around for ten years they had never been a cheap bike and were in demand not only from Wall riders but also from those interested in hill climbing. As a result, it wasn't unknown for someone riding a Scout in the street to be chased after by a Wall rider eager to get their hands on their machine, often offering them cash on the spot!

Postcards from as early as 1930 show Wall riders sitting astride Indian Scouts on the front of their Walls as well as riding round them. These pictures show flat-capped members of the public watching on with amazement at what they were witnessing beneath captions enticing them in such as 'Human Flies Cheating the Undertaker!' In these early years the shows were still evolving, but these same postcards show that proprietors were already showing inventiveness in their desire to be different, with evidence from very early on in the decade that they weren't confining themselves simply to bikes on the Wall: rudimentary cars were also being introduced.

Bikes still remained the number one attraction though and Indian Scouts not only held the specific advantages for Wall riders discussed in the previous chapter, but also had the allure of seeming just that bit different, more exotic somehow. Meanwhile individual riders were busy evolving their own styles and stunts on the bikes, and the adaptations referred to earlier were being experimented with during this period. Take the tank pad for example. Riders learned early on that a popular thing to do was to take a local member of the audience up on the tank of the bike, preferably a young lady. For the passenger this meant sitting on the tube running down the centre of the tank and on top of the oil pump plunger, a less than comfortable position, which meant that a solution was required. An early response was simply to put a towel or some rags down on the pad, but this was less than perfect as it allowed the passenger to slide around. The earliest evidence of a more permanent solution comes from photos of German riders, who fixed a leather pad over the top of the tank, often held in place with a strap. It wasn't long before this solution was adopted by UK riders who had seen this approach whilst working in Germany at the Oktoberfest.

Photographs from this era also give clues as to the styles and tricks of different riders, showing the handlebars on their bikes. Some handlebars were straight whilst others were curved backwards like a bicycle's. Wide handlebars suggested that the rider didn't perform the popular trick of sitting over the front of the handlebars as getting to this point required lifting a leg over the bars, and this wouldn't have been possible if they were too wide. More likely, wide handlebars might suggest the rider liked to take a passenger up on the Wall, as narrow bars would naturally restrict the room for getting their arms around the passenger whilst retaining the ability to steer the machine.

Many of the photos still extant from this period take the form of old postcards, which were a popular tool used by Wall riders at this time as publicity material, with insets of their faces framed by a tyre, usually set against a wider scene of them performing their trademark stunt on a Wall. Sometimes these cards were signed, which gives us an indication of the sort of status Wall riders enjoyed at the time, namely that of local, or even occasionally national, celebrities. Examples included here include Ken Hood, 'Cyclone' Jack Cody and the Perry husband and wife team. In fact married couples were a common act, with Skid and Alma Skinner and the notorious 'Barney and Doris' other examples.

Part of the Wall aristocracy in the UK at this time were the Todd family who operated a number of travelling Walls, with the brothers George, Frank and Jack all having their own Walls. A fourth brother, Bob, was also involved briefly, if spectacularly, as one of the very few people ever to rollerskate around a Wall, towed by one of his brothers, as early as 1932, in Ramsgate. Other leading names at this time also included Elias Harris, who was a son-in-law of Pat Collins, who had been a Wall pioneer but was also perhaps the top showman of his day, in the Midlands of the country at least. The two Albert Evanses, Senior and Junior, were also leading Wall owner-proprietors as well as riders themselves, a common combination, along with the Barrys. Other riders, some of whom had their own Walls, included Cyclone Jack Cody, Harry Holland, Jake Messham, Roy Swift and a retinue of women including not only the women in the married couple acts but Patsie Dare, a very early rider, and Winnie Souter, who married George Todd.

Such was the popularity of the Wall it would be impossible to list all the riders around at this time, although the beginnings of a list of leading riders was included in our earlier book *Riding the Wall of Death* (Tempus 2006), but one British name that can't be left out is that of Tornado Smith, whose fame was fired as much by his talent for self-publicity as his undoubted talent on the Wall. Smith featured in Pathé newsreels of the time with his lion 'Briton', which he used to take up on the Wall, although his claim to be the first to do so does not stand up to scrutiny. The same can be said of his boast of being the first Wall owner to take a car up onto the Wall of Death, as we have seen this was something that had been achieved in the early days of the Wall, although it never quite caught on.

Outside Britain Germany was probably the most prolific in producing Wall riders, with names such as Kitty Mathieu, Kitty Müller, Pitt Löffelhardt and Georg Koch leading the field, although others also came from Holland and outside Europe in Africa and Asia, whose names have now been forgotten. US riders included Lucky Thibeault, Fearless Egbert and Gunboat Jackson – again a full list would be impossible to compile. For US-based riders getting hold of an Indian Scout was of course easier, some were even bought brand new, but it is interesting to note that almost without exception it was this bike that riders gravitated towards irrespective of their nationality. A feature of Wall riders was their willingness to travel to reach their audiences and a number of American riders made it across the Atlantic, whilst British riders in particular showed a willingness to tour Europe and Russia, with Robby Hayhurst an example of one of these.

As the 1930s drew to a close, however, such travel became an impossibility as the cloud of war hovered over the Continent, and before too long both shows and bikes across Europe had to be put into storage. In the US meanwhile, as we have seen, production of the Indian concentrated on military machines in particular the 741, an adaptation of the Scout, along with the military Chiefs. In the early years of the war the US defence industry bought up stocks of steel and aluminium to supply the Allied war effort, making production of bikes difficult, and in February of 1942 the government ordered the production of all bikes for domestic use to cease. Indian were unsuccessful in winning the contract to supply the US Army, losing out to the larger Harley Davidson mainly due to concerns by the government that the Wigwam had suffered from lack of investment in the preceding years. They were, however, successful in selling the 741s to other Allied armies where 500cc models were more popular, in time selling over 30,000 bikes to British, Canadian and Australian forces. As the war set in for what was to be a long haul, other than a few Walls featuring at state fairs in the US and the occasional 'Holiday at Home' fair staged by the UK government, the Wall of Death, and its association with the Indian motorcycle, was put into the deep freeze, its future like everyone's future, uncertain.

The Munich Oktoberfest featured as many as three Walls.

The Wall of Death had grabbed the public's imagination as early as 1929.

A nonchalant-looking Ken Hood going round the Wall.

Stratford on Avon 1931 – 'Human Flies Cheating the Undertaker'.

"Cyclone Jack Cody on "Wall of Death."

FEARLESS JEAN PERRY   CAPTAIN PERRY

CAPTAIN PERRY ON THE WALL

Above *left:* Cyclone Jack Cody, taking it up to the wire.

Above *right:* The husband-and-wife Perrys.

Right: Harry Holland on the bike he was to later give to Yvonne Stagg.

MOTOR OIL

To Yvonne
Best wishes
Good Luck
Harry H

Above: Using a bathing beauty to pull in the crowds! (Photo: Messham Archive).

Above left: Skid and Alma Skinner's Wall at Cosham, Hampshire 1939.

Left: The Wall at the outbreak of the Second World War.

Above left: The Famous Hell Drivers, complete with caged lion.

Above right: Jack Barry's Wall in Huddersfield, 1938.

Right: Tornado Smith was never shy of advertising himself and claiming to be an original.

THE ORIGINAL
WALL OF DEATH
FEATURING
TORNADO SMITH
AND
MARJORIE DARE,
is open at
BOXFORD "WHITE HART"
(for one more week only), on
**Wednesday 13th, Saturday 16th,
and Wednesday 20th November.**
At 3.30, 7, 8, 9 and 10.   [630p

Barney and Doris, husband and wife Wall riders.

A boiler-suited (with tie!) Otto performing in the open air.

Speedy Curly Lee and his tank rider Miss Ray James – note the beaded edge tyres.

Start them young!

CHAPTER 5

FROM HEROES TO ZERO ... AND YET

After six years of warfare Wall of Death riders looked to pick up where they'd left off – as public heroes of outdoor entertainment. At the outbreak of the war the Wall had cemented its position as an icon of the entertainment world in the UK by acting as the backdrop for a George Formby film called *Spare a Copper*. Ten years later, in 1950, it was as if nothing had changed. It featured again in a film called *There is Another Sun* starring Laurence Harvey, which in time was to be renamed *The Wall of Death* in recognition both of the Wall's pivotal role in the film and of the attraction's capacity to pull audiences into the theatre. This film seemed to confirm that the fascination the Wall had exerted before the war was still there, with sequences in the film performed by Jimmy Kynaston along with a young Tommy Messham, who joined his father Jake, on whose Wall scenes for the film were shot.

What was true in the UK was also the case elsewhere, with the Wall picking up where it had left off both in the US and Germany. The Munich Oktoberfest and Hamburg Domfest both featured Walls in the 1950s. Walls of Death were relatively solid structures and although showmen had been obliged to pack them away on the outbreak of war, it was a relatively simple matter to retrieve them and get back on the road once the war was over. This was in contrast to many other fairground attractions which required either parts, many of which had originally come from Germany, or restoration after half a decade of neglect.

Equally robust were the Indians used on the Walls, and although many of those who'd ridden them before the war reappeared, they began to be joined by a fresh generation of riders fresh back from fighting and often with good experience of handling bikes picked up from despatch riding and other similar roles. A good example of the old and the new coming together was the Roy Swift & Harry Holland double act, who were entertaining the crowds at Belle Vue, Manchester. Holland had been riding Walls before the war and had taken on Swift in 1947 after being impressed by his experience of jumping bikes over cars. It took a little while for things to really pick up though, with matters not helped by the post-war austerity and a terrible winter in 1946/47. Once again it was a set-piece celebration that was to bring the Wall of Death back to centre stage.

Like the 1924 British Empire Exhibition, which had featured the Death Ring, the 1951 Festival of Britain was designed to lift spirits and showcase British talent and expertise. A Wall of Death was a permanent installation at the Festival Pleasure Gardens in Battersea, featuring Frank Todd's *Hell Riders*. Todd had been a pre-war rider and had been touring Italy when war broke out, causing him to flee, leaving his Wall behind him. With the festival he was signalling that he was back in business. He was not the only one in his family to be earning his living with a Wall of Death. His brother George, another leading pre-war showman, had a Wall at 'Merrie England' in Ramsgate which he rode along with his wife 'Fearless' Winnie Souter. Other pre-war riders coming back onto the scene included Elias Harris, who'd served out the war as an aviation fitter in Southampton, and Eddy Monte who travelled a Wall with Pat Collins' fair. The Kursaal in Southend also started up again featuring Tornado Smith.

Back in civilian life, however, the production of domestic motorcycles had taken a while to pick up, with a pent-up demand now far outstripping supply. In the UK there was a long waiting list for new BSAs or Triumphs, but at the same time there were regular military auctions of war-surplus stocks, mainly held in Bicester, including motorcycles. Indians featured prominently – both brand new still-crated machines as well as used ones. Such was the surplus that American forces even resorted to burying stocks of brand new bikes and Jeeps in landfill sites rather than take them back across the Atlantic. At the same time quite literally tons of spares became available wrapped up in waxed paper. The bikes were bought by dealers who then proceeded to paint the bikes back to their original red, the buying public having had their fill of military green by that time, and sell them on to a bike-hungry public.

Two main dealers stood out: Marble Arch Motor Supplies Ltd, who covered the south, and Fred Fearnley Ltd in Manchester. An advert in a November 1948 edition of *Motor Cycling* magazine shows the cost of a new Indian, complete with 'a hundred mile an hour speedo' (!) for £98/10, with the same advert offering a comparable military Harley at £89, suggesting that the Indian carried a premium. A new engine could be bought complete with gearbox and carburettor for £14/10. As a footnote, Marble Arch's remaining stock of Indian spares was bought by the American Motorcycling Register in the 1970s in a deal negotiated by Tudor Rees, and were subsequently stored in a barn in Bristol before being made available to club members.

As mentioned earlier, in the US the Indian Motocycle Company was struggling to get going again. A Model 841 had been designed which was a 750cc, transverse V-twin, shaft-driven machine, but only a thousand of these were ever built. Although the army liked them they didn't place an order, and the design was finally taken up as the basis for Moto Guzzi machines. This, along with the split that had taken place earlier between manufacturing and distribution, effectively ended the Indian era as an independent company.

Following the closure of the factory in 1953 a demand continued for Indian parts, however, and the flame was kept alive during this time largely due to the efforts of Sammy Pierce, a motorbike racer before the war. He opened a dealership in Fresno, California, in 1957 selling British-made Indians, which were actually Royal Enfields with an Indian nameplate and had been built after the company had obtained the manufacturing licence when the Indian factory had closed. Pierce bought up all the Indian parts he could get his hands on, including at one point 17 tons of parts from the Western States Indian distributor. Pierce even designed his own bike, the Indian Rocket, using a combination of old Indian parts and fresh components he made himself, but it never went into production. He went on to establish 'American Indian', an enterprise centred on a 'Super Scout' made from NOS parts, which also included some special body parts and performance upgrades. He sold up in 1971 before spending the last ten years of his life acting as curator to the actor Steve McQueen's extensive motorcycle collection.

Back in the UK demand for the Wall of Death held up during the 1950s, with the Swift/Holland double act mentioned earlier continuing through this period. Holland became one of the few riders to master going round backwards with no hands. By the end of the decade things were beginning to change though as demand began to dip, enough for Swift to throw in his lot as a trapeze artist. Holland took his Wall into Europe before touring the south of England with some new partners. It is the Indian Holland rode during these times that modern-day rider Ken Fox rides today. Previously, Holland had sent this bike back to the UK from Australia, where he was then living, for rider Yvonne Stagg to use at Dreamland in Margate. This show, along with Holland's bike, was subsequently bought by rider/proprietor Peter Catchpole who ironically took them to Australia for a while before coming back to the UK.

It's been estimated that there were at least a dozen Walls in the UK around this time, not that many less than the seventeen recorded in the US, but this figure was considerably less than there had been before the war. Leading Wall names from this era included not only the Todds but Albert Evans, who came from another established fairground family; Tornado Smith; the Irish Barry family; Ron Miller, who had a Wall in New Brighton; Freddy Heywood; and Jake Messham. The Cripsey family were also running a Wall in Skegness.

Barry's also ran a Wall at Portrush in 1953 featuring Cyclone Jake Messham, Tony Daring, Skid Beaumont and May Hogan, an Irish girl aged just 18, which ran until the 1960s with a succession of riders. The Goosens, featured in the previous chapter, also continued to tour, principally in Ireland. However they retired in 1959 to run Esso service stations in Co. Kildare following a bad accident whilst working at Barry's in Portrush, when the frame of Ena's bike broke sending her cascading to the floor below. Although not badly hurt, Ena was shaken up by the experience, which appears to have provided a reason to get out while they were still winning.

The pre-war tradition of female riders continued in the 1950s. Mention has already been made of Winnie Souter, but others included Betty Ellis and Maureen Swift. Swift's real name was Kelly and living in Southend had exposed her to the Wall belonging to Tornado Smith, based at the Kursaal there. Having learnt to ride on Tornado's Wall she was given her own by her parents as an 18th birthday present, a move which led to her whole family becoming involved in running the show. The Wall didn't last long, being badly damaged in a fire, and Swift went on to ride in Germany where she married a local and 'retired' in 1958.

The number of licensed motorbikes on British roads more than doubled during the 1950s to around 1,500,000 as they remained the working man's transport of choice, but the end of the decade marked the beginning of a high point. Motorbike ownership plateaued in 1960, falling off more rapidly from 1965 as small affordable cars came onto the market. The age of consumerism had begun and it affected more than just bikes. Increasing affluence and choice, especially around leisure and holidays, meant a drift away from what had become traditional pursuits. It is from around this time that the traditional British seaside holiday, the resorts for which were a mainstay of many a permanent Wall of Death, fell into near-terminal decline. This was especially true of holiday camps such as Butlins, which had been particularly strong markets for the Wall, as people began to explore the possibilities of cheap charter flights and guaranteed sun on the Mediterranean.

At the same time, travelling fairs found it harder to make a living and many went out of business as the public began to regard such entertainments as old-fashioned. The increasing number of cars on the road also meant a need for more car parks and many of the sites, or gaffs, where travelling shows set up were concreted over or turned into shopping centres. With a more diversified economy the tradition of Wakes Weeks, when one-industry towns would effectively close down during the same week each year, also declined. Everything, it seemed, was conspiring against traditional showmen and the Wall of Death.

1965 was not only the year that marked the turning point for motorbikes in the UK, it was also seminal in that it was the year in which the iconic Wall of Death rider and owner Tornado Smith finally retired, selling his Wall to one of the women then riding for him, Yvonne Stagg. Smith has already featured in this book, notably his unique talent for self-publicity which had made him almost certainly the country's most famous Wall rider during the pre-war years. His bowing out from the stage can be seen as a pivotal point in the history of the Wall in the UK.

From this point on the number of Walls began to drop off, with the Evans family retiring from the business in the late 1960s, although they continued to dabble in it for a while afterwards. Before too long it was only the Messham family that travelled a Wall of Death with father and son Jake and Tommy each having their own Wall and visiting the various big fairs dotted around the country that could still support an annual visit from the attraction. These included the large regional events such as Nottingham Goose Fair, Hull Fair, Newcastle Town Moor and St Giles Fair in Oxford.

The decline wasn't confined to the UK. As the 1970s drew to a close in the US there was only one Motordrome still doggedly operating in the New England area, traditionally the home of the Wall, probably due to its association with the spiritual home of the Indian in Springfield. Walls continued to operate in the Low Countries and Germany, where Pitt's Sensation or *Todeswand* (German for Wall of Death) kept the flame alive with riders such as Kitty Mathieu and Herbert Wissinger proving particularly popular (France had always been keener on the Wall's close cousin, the Globe of Death). There were also occasional sightings in places such as the Far East and India, but they were beginning to be regarded as a curiosity rather than a mainstay of the outdoor entertainment scene.

In the UK following Jake Messham's retirement Tommy Messham had the last travelling Wall but other static Walls struggled on, including a second Wall owned by Messham at Southsea, one in Barry Island and the Cripsey Wall in Skegness. Tornado Smith's Wall was still owned by Yvonne Stagg in the mid-1970s and she even transferred it from Southend to Margate when the Kursaal closed in 1974, where she was joined by Allan Ford. Stagg's tale was to end in tragedy when her partner was murdered by her lover, a story which was to make the front page of the papers, with the resulting trauma leading to her suicide over the New Year of 1976/77. At around the same time Messham put both of his Walls into storage and turned his attentions to running a set of four abreast Gallopers at Chessington Zoo, and one by one all the remaining Walls closed down. Riders who wanted to stay with the Wall now needed to take their Indians abroad in places as far flung as Dubai, Iran and Russia, where there was even a concrete Wall in Gorky Park, Moscow. By the end of the 1970s there were no Walls left operating on a regular basis in the UK.

One man whose career spanned this period was Doug 'Mileaway' Murphy, a mild-mannered but extremely skilled rider based in Colne, Lancashire, living in a modest back-to-back terraced house where he kept his 500cc 1928 Scout in the living room. His story is typical of many of the stalwart riders of this period, plying his trade in both the UK and, in an annual pilgrimage, in Germany, where he rode not only at the Oktoberfest but also at the Stuttgart Volksfest and other similar fairs. Over one weekend in Bonn along with two other riders he recorded a total of sixty-five shows, with his personal contribution involving two acts per show. Murphy loved to ride the Wall and didn't care where he did it, the stickers on his beloved bike telling of trips to Hawaii, the US, Russia and Israel, where he was to set a world record for going round the Wall. His bike was even more travelled than he was and could boast of trips to Australia, Nigeria and Liberia. At the end of each season Murphy returned to his home in the north west of England and saw the winter out pumping petrol at a local service station, a routine he happily kept up for thirty-six years, finally retiring in 1982 just as the Wall was nearing its temporary demise in the UK. He had planned to write his memoirs, which would have made fascinating reading, but sadly he died of emphysema the following year, a common cause of death amongst Wall riders due to the amount of exhaust fumes they are forced to inhale during each show.

All was not totally lost, however. In 1979 a US Wall rider called Wayne Campbell bought the Wall he'd previously ridden from 1972-76 when it had been in the possession of Joe Boudreau of Ocean Grove, Massachusetts. Boudreau had had it built in 1962 as a replacement for the one his father had built in 1929, the last of three Walls he was to build in his lifetime. Campbell's new acquisition came complete with eight Indian Scouts, four of them 37-cubic inch models built between 1924 and 1927, the others being 45-cubic inch 1928 models. After two years spent on restoration, much of which was devoted to the bikes, although the Wall itself had required six rotten inches to be cut off all the

Top: Claude Rye of London, one of the largest stockists of Indians in the UK after the war.

A new Indian for less than £100!

Above: A 1950 advert for ex-War Department machines.

way round, Campbell went on the road with his Wall. In 1982 he was joined by a rider called Don Daniels who went on to buy Campbell's Wall two years later and, after twenty years travelling with the Wall, to pass it on to his sons, who continue to travel with it today under the name 'The Hell Riders'. For a time there were three Walls of Death in the US, one of which was ridden by a woman rider Samantha Morgan, who rode a 1931 Indian Scout and had been mentored by one of the greatest names in US Motordrome history, Sonny Pelaquin, from whom she learned to ride at the tender age of 15. She went on to become a legend on the US circuit and died in 2008 aged only 53 from complications from the various injuries she'd picked up during her career.

Back in the UK a similar story of Walls being kept alive by a handful of enthusiasts also began to unfold. In the mid-1980s Allan Ford saw a Wall advertised in the fairground newspaper *World's Fair*, and recognising that this could be the chance of a lifetime he took a gamble and bought it. It was the Wall once run by the Cripsey family in Skegness and it needed a fair bit of attention to bring it back to operating condition as it had stood idle for a number of years. Over the course of a year, and drawing upon the efforts of friends and enthusiasts, the Wall was duly restored to a state where it could go on the road. It enjoyed its first outing at a steam rally at Blindley Heath near Godstone.

Over the next couple of years Ford was able to show that the public still had an appetite to watch the thrills and spills of the Wall. The economy had picked up from its bad times at the turn of the 1970s and the Wall of Death had been transformed from something almost passé to a curiosity. It was during this period that riders such as Chris Lee and Ned Kelly, who'd joined Ford as a lorry driver but took to the Wall, introduced the Wall to a fresh generation. Such was Ford's success that others soon got in on the act, but it was his Motordrome Company that stayed the course, lasting until the turn of the Millennium, when a combination of a very poor summer weather-wise and unfavourable economics caused him to 'pull in' and become a pub landlord. Towards the end of his time he'd been joined on the road by Ken Fox, who for a while had ridden with the Motordrome Company, and whilst others have come and gone in the meantime it has been Fox who has successfully picked up Ford's mantle and kept the Wall of Death flame alive, with his show, The Ken Fox Troupe, still operating to this day.

More recently, in 2008 Fox bought Tommy Meesham's Wall off Chris Palmer who had travelled with it for a couple of years after buying it off Roy Cripsey, and it is this Wall that is now travelled by Luke Fox, Ken's son. In the meantime, the Messham family has revived their own Wall, with three brothers coming together to put a show on the South Coast. And so it is that the grand old tradition of Wall showmanship passing through the blood is maintained, and the torch that keeps the Wall of Death alive is prepared for passing on to the next generation.

A 741B Military Indian on the rollers immediately after the war (Photo: Messham Archive).

Crowds still being drawn to the Wall in 1940, Sutton-in-Ashfield, Nottinghamshire.

Harry Holland and Roy Swift at Belle Vue, Manchester 1945.

Above Right: Spieling in the 1950s, Sweden.

Above: Albert Evans coming down from a dip.

Right: The Wall re-emerging after the war, in this case in Straford-upon-Avon.

Above: Roy Swift and Harry Holland with their bright-red shirts.

Above left: Jimmy Kynaston (left) going under the name of Boston Bob, along with Jake Messham and one other rider.

Left: A big crowd at the Oktoberfest in the 1950s.

Roy Swift with a female spieler. Note the mike!

Top: Watch the hat! Majorie Dare on Tornado Smith's Wall in Southend.

Above: German rider William Arne displaying his repertoire of tricks.

A car being readied for the Wall.

Pitt's Sensation, the German *Todeswand* or Wall of Death.

Cliff Ellis with a sidecar attached to an Indian 101.

Cliff Ellis trick riding. Note the twin safety cable as required in Germany.

Doug Murphy
Israel 1963 - 64 - 65

Above left: One of Tommy Messham's bikes used on the rollers in 1971.

Above right: A signed postcard showing Doug Murphy riding in Israel in the 1960s.

Right: How many people can you fit on an Indian?

Above: Bikes awaiting shipment to Australia from Dreamland including Harry Holland's. Sadly most never made the return trip.

Left: Harry Holland's bike on returning to the UK for use by Yvonne Stagg.

Harry Holland's bike after being restored by
Allan Ford.

The early days of the Motordrome Company (1987), one of the trick bikes that came
with the Wall – note the Honda hub.

Allan Ford trick rider as part of the Motordrome Company in the 1980s.

Above: A young Chris Lee riding the rollers on Messham's Wall, note the framework at the rear to allow the rider to stand on the rear wheel spindle footrest.

Above left: Chris Lee performing side-saddle as part of the Motordrome Company.

Left: Ned Kelly performing on the rollers on the Pitt's Wall in Munich, Germany, late 1990s.

Above: The Cripsey's 101s. Note how the frame has been shortened.

Below: Doug Murphy's own trick bike. Note the throttle cable from right hand twist grip and small petrol tank under seat, with a list of places the rider has ridden on the rear.

A 101 with a shortened frame on the rollers (1987).

Above left: Inside a German Wall. Note the unusual tank pad.
Above right: A selection of German Walls from the 1970s.

Left: The German rider Herbert Wissinger in action.

Above: Cliff Ellis's trick bike – even the chain is painted red!

Right: Cliff and Betty Ellis at the Oktoberfest 1960, with Betty on the sidecar.

Right: A section of Kitty Mathieu's Wall now in a museum in Munich.

The front of Tommy Messham's Wall with a nice line of Indians on display.

Above: Allan Ford in action on his Wall, literally taking it to the wire.

Above right: Ken Fox in action in the 1990s.

Right: Tommy Messham junior prepares to sell his bikes to Allan Ford.

Luke Fox riding on the handlebars.

A girl being taken for a ride around James Messham's Wall of Death.

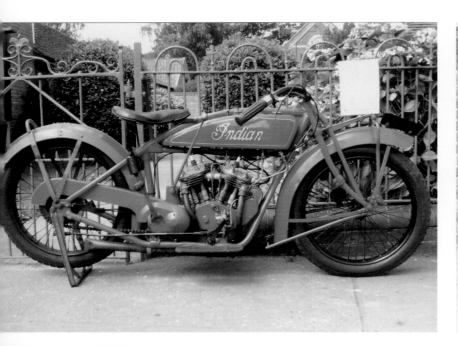

Above left and right: Two road Indians … spot the difference – handlebars, silencers, fenders, saddle brackets, footbrake levers, rear carriers, control cables, fork links, dynamos, lights!

A restored 101 with sloping foot boards.

CHAPTER 6

THE SPIRIT LIVES ON

In the same way that the Wall of Death has proven, to borrow from Mark Twain's famous quote, that reports of its death have been greatly exaggerated, the same is true of the Indian motorcycle. Back in the US the old Indian Motocycle Company had finally expired in 1953, but in 1998 a number of previously competing companies came together to form a new company to carry the Indian name, resolving what had been a tangled web of trademark disputes around the company's name. Manufacturing began the next year but the venture failed to get out of second gear, and in 2003 the new Indian Motorcycle Company (this time with an 'r' in the name) folded. The mantle was then picked up by Stephen Julius and Steve Heese who acquired the trademark rights and intellectual property in 2004 and, in 2008, production began on a 2009 Indian Chief from assembly lines in Kings Mountain North Carolina.

New Indian President Julius runs a private equity firm that specialises in resurrecting famous brands, and professed as production re-started that he saw the challenge before him as a ten, fifteen or even twenty-year project. His partner Heese meanwhile acts as Chairman of the new company and made his name in the global construction parts industry before linking up with Julius to revive the Chris-Craft boat company based in Florida. It is early days for the new company, but whether or not it meets its new owners' ambitions is probably irrelevant when it comes to keeping the Indian name alive. The soul of the company remains lodged firmly in the old 1920s Scouts that were and are the bike of choice for the Wall of Death rider. Indeed, it's probably fair to say that that there are more of these bikes in working order, and in good working order at that, today than there have been since the heyday of the Wall of Death.

Whereas in the 1960s and 70s Indians spinning round the boards were held together with a combination of insulating tape, wire and a touch of good old showman's 'bodge' – a tribute to the inherent robustness of the basic design of the machine – these days the working bikes are better maintained than perhaps they have ever been. Furthermore, others have been found or rescued and been put back into road trim with mudguards and lights, something some riders view as a shame or possibly even a sacrilege, turning what had been an honest working machine into a showpiece, rarely even ridden.

There are a number of factors driving this development, but at the heart of them all is the enduring popularity of the Indian and the affection it holds in many people's hearts. Very few marques enjoy this degree of mystique and following, something which sets Indian apart – it is worthy of note for example that no lesser collector than the late actor Steve McQueen chose to focus on Indians for his motorbike collection. Particularly significant has been the formation of active Indian riders' clubs in many of the countries where the bike was popular. A list of current clubs is featured overleaf. The essence of these clubs and their members seem to capture something it is difficult to articulate, something that the Indian seems to encapsulate that for enthusiasts sets it apart from other brands, a sort of spirit that seems to say that anyone can ride a Harley, but it takes an expert to ride an Indian. The Indian clubs act both as a forum for the exchange of information – something that has been made easier by the internet – and indirectly also provide a marketplace. This marketplace involves both a growing cottage industry of people trading existing parts and spares and those making patterns for cylinders and crank cases and manufacturing new spares and components.

Once again, trading has been made easier by the internet and whereas Indian clubs once kept the flame alive in individual countries, trading now has a distinctly international flavour.

INDIAN MOTORCYCLE CLUBS AROUND THE WORLD

COUNTRY	CLUB	CONTACT
Australia	Indian Motocycle Owners' Club, Australia	info@indianmotocycle.info
Austria	Austrian Indian Riders	florian.faltin@chello.at
Belgium	Indian Friends, Belgium	indianrolly@hotmail.com
Canada	Indian Club Canada	
Denmark	Indian Club Denmark	super.carla@mail.tele.dk
Finland	Indian Club of Finland	virtakai@saunalahti.fl
Germany	Indian Motorcycle Club Germany	hg340el@uni-duisburg.de
Great Britain	Indian Riders of Great Britain	clubsecretary@indianriders.co.uk
Great Britain	Indian Motocycle Club of Great Britain	jdwright@netcomuk.co.uk
Italy	Registro Storico Italiano Indian	info@indianmotorcycle.it
Netherlands	Indian Motorcycle Club Netherlands	altjo@indian.nl
New Zealand	Indian Owners' Register New Zealand	wads@orcon.co.nz
Norway	Indian Club Norway	stf@c2i.net
Poland	Oldtimer Club Poland	oldtimerclub@riders.pl
Slovenia	Indian MC of Slovenia	muzej.motociklov@siol.net
Sweden	Swedish Indian Society	jostrand@algonet.se
Switzerland	Indian Rider Association Switzerland	mail@iras.ch
US	All American Indian Club	jrk53@aol.com
US	The 101 Association	rwmc101@aol.com
Czech Republic	Indian Motocycle Club Czech Republik	indian@flat4.org

The enthusiasm and expertise of those who have taken it upon themselves to specialise in all things Indian seems to reflect the spirit kept alive by the Indian clubs. Mention has already been made of 'Mr Indian', Sammy Pierce, who almost single-handedly championed Indians in the immediate post-war period in the US, but his passion and enthusiasm has been replicated then and since by others in both the UK and Europe. Some specialise in parts, whilst for others it is all about restoration.

Two names stand out in Holland for example: the Pelders and Tony Leenes. The Pelders make and sell virtually every part for an Indian and started by manufacturing reproduction motorcycle transfers twenty years ago. After buying their own veteran Indian motorcycle they caught the bug and moved into the production and sales of Indian parts, and now travel all over the world to different Swap Meets and Auto-Jumbles with their stall. Tony Leenes supplies spares and builds machines and founded the Indian Motorcycle Museum in his hometown of Lemmer, Friesland.

In the UK the list goes on and those worthy of particular mention include Mike de Bidalph, who along with his wife Sybil runs the Indian Riders' Club of Great Britain. Mike bought his first Indian from Marble Arch Motor Stores in 1947 after being demobbed in 1946 having worked on landing-ship tank craft and minesweepers as a Petty Officer Motor Mechanic (POMM) in the engine rooms. He has owned most models made from the 1920s and has ridden Indians all over the world, even importing Indian Chiefs from Chile and Argentina in 1993. As well as his duties to the Indian Riders' Club of Great Britain, Mike now spends most of his time restoring Indians.

Another UK-based Indian hero is Alan Gould, who runs Roberts Bridge Motorcycles. Alan saw his first Indian in 1981 whilst working on his Plymouth Superbird. Ten years later he wanted a motorbike for the road so it had to be an Indian. He now owns a motorcycle and cycle shop in Roberts Bridge, Kent, maintaining a family tradition as his grandfather had a garage and worked on Indians in Ireland before the war. The Roberts Bridge premises had been used as a motorcycle shop for over 100 years and since taking it over in 2008 Alan has restored a 750cc Daytona Scout amongst other machines. His premises are an Aladdin's Cave and well worth a visit.

Carol and Ray Cris also deserve a mention. Based in Sussex, Ray is a classic example of an Indian collector, whilst his wife Carol is the foremost restorer of Indian saddles in the country if not the world, using only the top-quality, oak bark-tanned, English cowhide and hand-made thread in her work. Someone else instrumental in keeping the spirit alive in the UK is Alan Forbes, who is based in Edinburgh and was the singer with the punk band The Rezillos where his stage name was Eugene Reynolds. More recently he created Indian Motorcycles UK Ltd. Although this doesn't claim to be linked to the US company, it does manufacture parts and get involved in restoring old vintage Indians.

It is every trick rider's dream to own his or her own machine, and one whose dream has recently come true is Ned Kelly, a rider who learned to ride with Allan Ford in the 1980s and went on to work for Ken Fox/Peter Catchpole before riding in Germany for Hugo Dabbert. After hanging up his boots he set up a Government Surplus Shop in Pontypridd, South Wales, but he never gave up on owning his own trick bike. His chance came when he heard of a frame and a box of parts from Mike de Bidalph which had, as they say 'some potential'. He duly parted with his cash and started scouring the world for missing parts, advertising in the various Indian club magazines and surfing the internet. His is a very modern story, tapping into the goodwill of the international Indian community. The bike is taking shape quickly with Ned being able to buy new parts from dealers such as the Pelders and Alan Gould. A feature of the bike is that it uses 741 barrels, cams and pistons, suitably modified by Mike de Bidalph. Luck has played its part too, with Ned spotting a pair of Indian handlebars hanging in someone's shed in Wales. The whole enterprise has taken a combination of patience and perseverance but it won't be long before another Indian Wall of Death trick bike will be brought back to life.

There are plenty of others involved in Indian parts and restoration, often specialising in particular parts, such as magnetos or wheels, with a good example of the latter being Wheelwise, based in West Sussex. It shouldn't be forgotten for example that UK Wall of Death rider and owner of two Walls, Ken Fox, is also an expert restorer and builds and maintains his own machinery in his extensive workshop. Another restorer of special distinction is Charles Winter from Surrey, who has been around the Indian and Wall of Death and Globe of Death scene in the UK for over thirty years, including being a trick rider with each. Charles has been involved in restoring a number of Indians during that time, with three of them especially worthy of mention.

The first of these is a 1923 Indian Scout, which was first used on the Wall in the days of Cyclone Jake Messham and Jimmy Kynaston in the 1950s, both of whom used the bike regularly. Subsequently it passed to Tommy Messham's Wall, where it was ridden by Chris Lee. The bike wasn't used for a number of years until it was seen with Gerry de Roy, who rode it on the ex-Albert Evans Wall at Southsea in the early 1980s. Charles Winter subsequently learned to trick ride on it and rebuilt it in the latter part of that decade. The restored bike was ridden in Singapore by him and Ken Fox to support Tommy Messham Junior, by which time its tyres were over forty years old and left great black marks on the Wall as a result of the heat in which it was ridden. The Messham connection continues to this day, the bike being passed to Jake Messham by Charles Winter whilst working in South Korea in 2006-07. Those who ride it say it is a well-balanced bike and one of the most comfortable rides they've had. It is distinguished by its unusual design of tank pad and the leather belt on the front forks, there as a safety feature just in case the leaf spring breaks.

The second bike is a 1924 Scout first used on the Wall by pre-war rider Eddie Monte. It was restored by Charles Winter who believes it is the only known original Tornado Smith bike still in working order. When Monte sold his Wall and bikes to Tommy Messham the bike needed quite a lot of work, largely on account of what Messham described as Monte's preference to have a 'loose' set up, by which he meant worn out! It's worth mentioning that at their peak the Messham family had over thirty Indian Scouts in their stable. Today around half that number remain, with some having found their way back to their homeland in the US where they are prized exhibits as original Wall of Death or Silodrome machines.

The third bike, a 1926 model, was Cyclone Jake Messham's original trick bike, used up and down the country and in Ireland for decades on what was known by the family as 'the Big Wall'. This was also the bike ridden by Jake in the film *There is Another Sun*. One day in the late 1970s Jake invited his grandson Tommy Junior into the workshop in his yard in Haymills Birmingham where he kept all his equipment. He pulled at the corner of a dirty tarpaulin sheet to unveil a dusty red motorcycle and turning to young Tommy he exclaimed 'I won't be using this any more and I've heard that you are learning to trick ride on your Dad's Wall, so this is now for you.' It was an emotional moment for the old showman and his grandson. Young Tommy went on to ride the bike for many years having taken over the ownership of his father's Wall until he sold up in the mid-1990s.

In 2008 the bike was repainted at short notice by showman's decorator D.C. Slater. It was transported to Rhyl in North Wales and placed outside the church where thousands of people had gathered to pay tribute to young Tommy at his funeral, where his life of thrills and spills on and off the Wall was remembered with affection. Today it is used by James, Jake junior and Nathan Messham on their Wall around the UK and Ireland, keeping the family tradition going.

In the meantime there are others proudly keeping the Indian spirit alive on the Wall of Death. Mention has already been made of Luke Fox, a second-generation Wall rider, but he is not alone, with his brother also now trick riding on his father's Wall. As we have seen, the Messham family was synonymous with the Wall in the 1970s and James Messham has recently revived the family tradition by travelling a Wall originally built by Luke's father Ken. More recently, Allan Ford's old Wall, which was rotting away in Sussex, has returned home to the Evans family which originally owned it, with Albert Evans junior already having a nicely restored Indian ready to ride on it.

All this seems to go to show how the Indian spirit, and the link between these unique bikes and the Wall of Death, seems to refuse to die. Walls may go into storage and riders may retire, but there always seems to be people prepared to accept the passing of the baton, to rebuild a Wall or restore a bike, or better still to do both and become the next generation of Indian Heroes trying to wear out their Indian Scout!

Alan Gould outside his shop.

Mike de Bidaph assembling an Indian clutch.

A completed restoration of one of Tommy Messham's trick bikes.

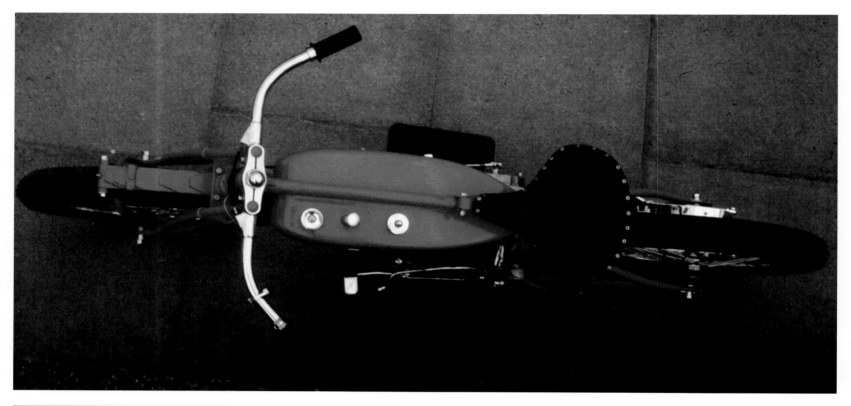

Above: Top view of a restored bike.

Left: Basket case?

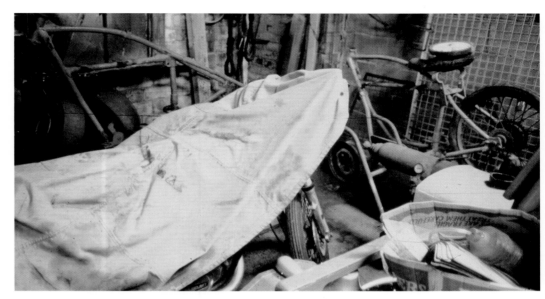

Remains of Indians left in a showman's yard.

Aces High!

Above left: Taking shape.

Above right: Finding out just what's missing.

Right: Anthony Harris' Wall bike, a winner in the vintage class at the Bulldog Bash 2007.

Opposite: Carol Cris at work restoring an Indian saddle.

Fitting 741 barrels.

Problems with a re-sleeved barrel.

Wall legend Gerry de Roy signing the tank of Albert Evans' motorcycle.

This tattoo shows how Indians can get under the skin.

Above: Steve Rolfe of wheelbuilding specialists Wheelwise.

Opposite: The Pelders with their Indian parts at an Auto-Jumble.

Left: Got any scrap metal Mister?

Above: From humble beginnings …

Far left: Claude and Rolland van Gysell who run the Belgian Indian riders' club, Indian Friends, seen here at an Auto-Jumble at Ludwigshafen, Germany.

Left: Jurgen Mattern, a 741 parts specialist, a member of the German Indian riders' club, the largest in Europe.

Wall of Death Indian restored.

Above: Just some of the many magazines available on Indians over the years.

Opposite: Ray Cris, another member of the tribe of Indian enthusiasts, keeping the spirit alive.

Above: Ken Fox sitting on Harry Holland's old bike, now Ken's trick bike.

Above right: Nicely restored

Right: Wall of Death Indian restored to full road trim.

Opposite page: A pride of Indians on Tommy Messham's front in the 1980s. (Photo: Charles Winter)

Above: This machine spent most of its life on the Wall of Death but now tours bike shows.

Top left: An unusual German bike with boxed in forks, right-hand cable-twist grip, Japanese wheel hubs and exhaust pipe. Note screw adjuster on the front link.

Left: A German Wall of Death bike with exceptionally long exhaust pipes.

Close up of timing side showing the way the dynamo is driven off the clutch gear.

Jake Messham's Indian, restored by Charles Winter.
(Photo: Charles Winter)

Eddie Monte's Indian, restored by Charles Winter. (Photo: Charles Winter)

Rock on Tommy Messham junior. (Photo: Charles Winter)

The three Messham brothers with two of James Messham's Indians.

The numberplate says it all!